Threads of History

A Thematic Approach to Our Nation's Story for AP* U.S. History

by Michael Henry, Ph.D.

To the Memory of My Parents:
Gleason and Dorothy Henry

Publisher: David Nazarian
Editor: Richard Carson
Cartographer: Sal Esposito

The publisher would like to thank Dan Frederiks, U.S. History teacher extraordinaire.

Cover Image: Map Quilt (detail); Artist unidentified; Possibly Virginia, 1886; Silk and cotton with silk embroidery; 78 3/4 x 82 1/4"; Collection American Folk Art Musuem, New York; Gift of Dr. and Mrs. C. David McLaughlin; 1987.1.1; Photo by Schecter Lee, New York

Image Credits: p. 22, Camp Meeting at Eastham, MA, Boston Athenæum, Boston, MA; p. 48, "The Grange Awakening the Sleepers," The Granger Collection, New York City; p. 64, "Hands Off!" from Puck Magazine, 1906; p. 90, "A Squelcher for Women's Suffrage," from Puck Magazine, 1894; p. 94, cartoon by CK Berryman from The Evening Star, 1919, Library of Congress; p. 130, cartoon by CK Berryman from The Washington Star, 1935; p. 138, cartoon by Roy Justus from the Minneapolis Star, 1947; p. 142, photograph by Paul Richards, 1969, Harvey Richards Media Archive; p. 165, The introduction of African slavery into the American colonies at Jamestown, Virginia, August, 1619, wood engraving, late 19th century, The Granger Collection, New York City; p. 171, cartoon of the Ninth National Women's Rights Convention, May 12, 1859, Harper's Weekly, June 11, 1859; p. 177, "A Giant Straddle," by William Allen Rogers, Harper's Weekly, March 28, 1896;

* AP is a registered trademark of the College Board, which was not involved in the production of, and does not endorse, this product.

Common Core State Standards © Copyright 2010. National Governors Association Center for Best Practices and Council of Chief State School Officers. All rights reserved.

ISBN 978-0-9905471-0-5

Copyright © 2015
Sherpa Learning, LLC.
West Milford, New Jersey
www.sherpalearning.com

All rights reserved. No part of this book may be kept in an information storage or retrieval system, transmitted or reproduced in any form or by any means without prior written permission of the Publisher.

Printed in the United States of America.

10 9 8 7 6 5 4 3 2 1

Threads of History
2nd Edition

Preface

    Thinking Like a Historian v

    Using *Threads of History* v

    Threads Walk-Through vi

Review & Source Activities

Lesson 1:	Historical Periods	2
Lesson 2:	Famous Rebellions	6
Lesson 3:	Religious Development, 1619–1740	10
Lesson 4:	Presidents of the United States, 1789–2001	14
Lesson 5:	The First and Second Great Awakenings	20
Lesson 6:	Coming of the American Revolution	24
Lesson 7:	The National Banks	28
Lesson 8:	*Liberal* and *Conservative* in United States History, 1790–1940	32
Lesson 9:	*Liberal* and *Conservative* in United States History, 1940–1985	36
Lesson 10:	Political Parties in the Nineteenth Century	40
Lesson 11:	Third Parties in United States History	45
Lesson 12:	Freedom of the Seas and Wars with Europe	50
Lesson 13:	Compromises and the Union	54
Lesson 14:	Judicial Nationalism, 1819–1824	58
Lesson 15:	Cornerstones of United States Foreign Policy	62
Lesson 16:	Expansion of the United States, 1783–1853	66
Lesson 17:	Wars in United States History	71
Lesson 18:	Amendments to the Constitution	76
Lesson 19:	Utopian Societies in the 1830s and 1840s	79
Lesson 20:	Expanding Democracy—The Abolitionist Movement	84

Lesson 21:	Women's Movement during the Nineteenth Century	88
Lesson 22:	Major Treaties in United States History	92
Lesson 23:	Reconstruction of the South	96
Lesson 24:	Judicial Betrayal—The Road to *Plessy v. Ferguson*	100
Lesson 25:	Monetary Policy—Gold vs. Silver, 1862–1900	104
Lesson 26:	Social Darwinism vs. the Social Gospel Movement	108
Lesson 27:	Black Leaders, 1880–1968	112
Lesson 28:	The Supreme Court and Government Regulation, 1890–1937	116
Lesson 29:	Reform Movements of the Twentieth Century	120
Lesson 30:	Isolationism vs. Internationalism, 1919–1941	124
Lesson 31:	Transformation of Capitalism in the 1930s	128
Lesson 32:	Presidential Civil Rights Records, 1945–1974	132
Lesson 33:	Containment, 1945–1975	136
Lesson 34:	Failure of Containment—The Vietnam War	140
Lesson 35:	Famous Doctrines—from Monroe to Nixon	144

Appendices

- **A.** Answer Key for Multiple-Choice Questions 150
- **B.** Distribution Charts
  - Items by Chronological Period 152
  - Items by Learning Objective 153
  - Items by Historical Thinking Skill 153
  - Applying the Common Core State Standards© 154
- **C.** Worksheets for Primary Sources
  - Document Source Analysis 156
  - Visual Source Analysis 157
  - Map Analysis 158
- **D.** The Mini-Reader 160
  - Note to Teachers and Adminstrators 166

Threads of History
2nd Edition

Preface

Thinking Like a Historian

This book was constructed with one distinct aim: to help you to develop *historical habits of the mind*. You might ask, "Shouldn't the aim be to help me score a 5 on the AP U.S. History exam?" In truth, those are one and the same.

Traditional "test prep" is designed to do one thing and one thing only—to cram a ton of information into your brain as quickly as possible. And yet, the AP U.S. History exam is not about how many U.S. history facts you can recall correctly; rather, it is designed to see if you have developed the skills needed to think like a historian. The test in 2015 and beyond will require that you surpass the literal understanding of the information given to create systematic relationships between facts, assess the reliability of information, identify point of view in sources, and recognize the connections of facts to larger historical concepts. Those are the historical habits of the mind that you will develop over the course of this year, and that will be necessary for success on both the exam in May and in your college years to come.

Although you will be required to develop these higher level thinking skills, your reasoning about United States history must still have a factual foundation. You cannot think historically unless you have accurate historical information from which to form your thoughts! Facts about people, ideas, and organizations are still necessary to succeed in AP U.S. History. While you must know specific information for the course, knowing the content cannot be an end in itself. That content must serve as a vehicle to develop broader ideas, concepts, and generalizations. The resources in *Threads of History*, along with your textbook, lectures, and class discussions, serve as the raw material to help you connect facts and to establish new patterns of meaning and understanding about America's past.

Using *Threads of History*

The book may be used in several ways. Your teacher may supply each member of the class with a copy of the book and use it as part of your regular classroom instruction and review. In this case, your teacher will determine the method of instruction and the frequency with which you utilize **Threads**. On the other hand, if **Threads** is part of your independent study program, you should examine two or three lessons at a time and answer the multiple-choice and short answer questions that accompany both the charts and the source materials.

Keep in mind that the lessons in *Threads of History* are designed as review activities. They are meant to be a useful companion to your primary textbook by providing concise summaries of broad themes and concepts that are scattered throughout the survey course. You should not expect detailed explanations about terms, people, or events. If you see terms or topics that you do not know, go to your textbook or your teacher to find out information about them.

Threads Walk-Through

Review Activities

The **Introduction** establishes the historical context of the topic or theme of each lesson.

The **Charts** synthesize historical data on the topic or theme. While the charts supply factual connections on topics that will be presented in your AP class, they also help establish deeper understanding of historical material.

The **Multiple-Choice** questions test your comprehension of the data presented in the charts.

Lesson 31: Transformation of Capitalism in the 1930s

The New Deal was Franklin Roosevelt's plan to restore economic prosperity to the United States during the 1930s. Though Roosevelt expanded the powers of the federal government enormously from 1933 to 1939 and alleviated the suffering of millions of Americans, his economic programs failed to end the Depression. It would take the Second World War to accomplish that.

Roosevelt's program to alleviate the Depression had two distinct phases. A First New Deal from 1933 to 1935 concentrated on economic relief and recovery and attempted to establish a government partnership with American corporations and businesses. A Second New Deal from 1935–1939 focused on long-term reforms in the American economy and took a confrontational stance toward the business community and the wealthy by imposing higher taxes and new, stricter regulations.

The chart on the next page outlines the basic differences between the First and Second New Deals. As you study it, consider the factors that undermined cooperation between big business and the government. Further, in what ways did the First and Second New Deals attempt to alter the capitalist system?

Directions: Analyze the chart on the First and Second New Deals, and then answer the following questions.

1. During the First New Deal, Franklin Roosevelt believed
   (A) the National Recovery Administration should nationalize the major industries
   (B) corporations that provided public services must accept government regulations and limitations on their profits
   (C) businessmen should be left alone to make as much money as possible
   (D) the government must cooperate with the business community to lift the country out of the Depression

2. In the Second New Deal, the government's attitude toward wealthy Americans was that
   (A) the gap between the wealthy and other classes should be narrowed through taxing policy
   (B) rich people should be protected because their spending could stimulate prosperity
   (C) the incomes of all Americans should be roughly equal
   (D) inherited wealth hurt the country and prolonged the depression

3. The primary g...
   (A) to control...
   economic...
   (B) to provid...
   Depressi...
   (C) to break...
   since the...
   (D) to establi...
   America'...

	First New Deal	Second New Deal
Dates	1933–1935	1935–1939
Goals	Direct relief to unemployed; recovery from the Depression	Revived progressive tradition of trust regulation
	Cooperated with business community to restore pre-1929 prosperity	Strengthened organized labor
	Helped organized labor to improve position in society	Sought to meet needs of workers, elderly, disabled, farmers, unemployed
	Provided assistance to agriculture	Narrowed class differences by taxing the wealthy
		Supported industrial workers and small farmers
Position on Business	Partnership	Confrontational toward corporate interests
	Cooperation	Strong regulation of public utilities
	Suspended Antitrust actions	
Actions	National Industrial Recovery Act	Public Utility Holding Company Act
	Agricultural Adjustment Act	Wealth Tax Act (Revenue Act)
	Federal Emergency Relief Act	National Labor Relations Act (Wagner Act)
	Emergency Banking Act	Works Progress Administration
	Civilian Conservation Corp	Social Security Act
	Tennessee Valley Authority Act	Fair Labor Standards Act
Comments	Brief honeymoon between business community and the Roosevelt administration	Stronger controls and higher taxes on the wealthy and large businesses
	First New Deal told business what it must do	Responded to attacks by Liberty League and Supreme Court's judicial review
	Business found New Deal regulations increasingly confining and intrusive	Second New Deal told business what it must *not* do
	Supreme Court sided with business interests as it struck down several major New Deal acts	

Source Activities

Accompanying each of the charts are **Primary Sources**, including document excerpts, cartoons, paintings, maps, and photographs, that correspond to the topic or theme of the lesson. These sources and the exercises connected to them will introduce and develop the historical thinking skills necessary for success in AP U.S. History.

Source Activities

Directions: Using the cartoon below and your knowledge of American history, answer the following questions.

The Washington Star, June 2, 1935

Multiple-Choice

1. The ideas expressed in the cartoon most directly reflect which of the following continuities in United States history?
   (A) debates over the role of the federal government in economic matters
   (B) debates over the transportation system that best suited the nation
   (C) debates over presidential power to amend the Constitution
   (D) debates over the role of the federal government in religious matters

2. The question highlighted in the cartoon was raised earlier in the twentieth century when the federal government began to
   (A) desegregate the schools in the South
   (B) provide health care for immigrant groups
   (C) establish a uniform currency in the United States
   (D) regulate corporation business practices

Short-Answer

Using the cartoon, answer a, b, and c.

a) Briefly explain how ONE of the following individuals would react to the ideas expressed in the cartoon:
   • Harry Hopkins
   • Norman Thomas
   • Herbert Hoover

b) Briefly explain how ONE of the remaining individuals would challenge the response of the individual selected in part a.

c) Briefly explain ONE example of how President Roosevelt sought to implement the point of view expressed in the cartoon from 1933–1941.

Multiple-Choice and Short-Answer questions are designed to foster historical thinking skills by challenging you to analyze and evaluate the sources.

Lesson 31: Transformation of Capitalism in the 1930s - **131**

Threads Walk-Through

Distribution Charts

Appendix B — Distribution Charts

Time Periods	Chart & Chart Questions	Source Activities Multiple-Choice	Source Activities Short-Answer	LEQs & DBQs
1600–1754	2.3; 4.1, 2, 3; 5.2, 3	3.1	3.a, b, c	LEQ 1; DBQ 1
1755–1783	6.1, 2, 3; 16.2	6.1, 2	6.a, b, c	
1784–1815	2.2; 3.3; 7.1, 2; 8.1, 2; 10.1, 2; 12.1, 2; 13.1; 18.1	2.1, 2; 3.1, 2; 4.3; 7.2; 12.1, 2; 35.2	2.a, b; 4.a, b, c; 10.a; 12.a	LEQ 2, 3, 4, 8
1816–1837	2.1; 7.3; 13.2; 14.1, 2, 3; 15.1; 20.1, 2; 21.3, 22.1, 35.2	5.1; 10.1, 2; 14.1; 16.1; 25.2; 35.1	5.a, b, c; 7.a, b, c; 10.b; 14.a, b	LEQ 4
1838–1859	1.1; 10.3; 11.2, 3; 16.1, 3; 17.1; 20.3; 19.1, 2, 3; 21.1	5.2; 13.1, 2; 16.2; 18.2; 19.2; 20.1, 2; 21.2; 27.1	13.a, b, c; 16.a, b; 19.a, b, c; 20.a, b, c; 21.a, b	LEQ 4, 6, 8, 9, 16; DBQ 2
1860–1877	4.1, 2; 8.3; 13.3; 18.2; 23.1, 2, 3; 25.3	1.1, 2; 23.1, 2; 32.2	1.a, b, c; 23.a, b	
1878–1901	1.3; 11.1; 15.2, 3; 17.3; 21.2; 24.1, 2, 3; 25.1, 2; 26.1, 2, 3	7.1; 8.1, 2; 11.1, 2; 15.1; 24.1, 2; 25.1; 26.1	8.a, b; 11.a, b, c; 14.c; 23.c; 25.a, b	LEQ 8, 11, 17; DBQ 3
1902–1929	1.2; 12.3; 20.3; 27.3; 30.1, 2, 3; 28.1, 2, 3	15.2; 21.1; 22.1, 2; 28.1; 29.1; 31.2	8.c; 12.b; 15.a, b; 16.c; 21.c; 22.a, b; 26.a, b; 35.b	LEQ 11, 12, 17
1930–1953	8.1; 22.2; 29.2; 31.1, 2, 3; 33.1; 35.1	9.2; 17.1; 18.1; 26.2; 28.2; 30.1, 2; 31.1	15.c; 17.a, b, c; 22.c, 24.a, b, c; 29.a; 30.a, b, c; 31.a, b, c	LEQ 2, 5, 12, 13
1954–1972	8.2; 17.2; 18.3; 27.2; 29.1, 3; 32.1, 2, 3; 33.2, 3; 34.1, 2, 3	14.2; 17.2; 19.1; 27.2; 32.1; 33.1; 34.1, 2	9.b; 27.a, b, c; 29.b, c; 32.a, b, c; 33.a, b; 34.a, b, c	LEQ 14, 15
1973–1990	8.3; 35.3	9.1; 29.2; 33.2	9.a; 33.c	

To assist you further in assessing your overall readiness for the AP U.S. History examination, Appendix B contains a series of charts that connect the multiple-choice and short-answer items in the 35 lessons to vital categories and standards.

- The first chart (shown on the left) breaks down the items in the book into the 11 key chronological periods.

- The second and third charts break down the items by the standards set forth in the College Board's framework for the AP U.S. History course, including the Learning Objectives and the Historical Thinking Skills.

- The fourth chart connects the content of *Threads* to the Common Core State Standards for History/Social Studies for Grades 11–12.

You and your teacher can use the various charts to determine which of the Review Activity charts you understood and which topics need further study. Examine the patterns of missed questions carefully in making final preparations for the test.

- For example, if you had many errors in the content years 1607–1754, you should revisit lessons 2, 4, and 5, and review your textbook chapters and class notes that deal with the materials on the settlement of North America, colonial development, and the British and French conflicts to the eve of the French and Indian war in 1754.

- Or, if you find that you are struggling with questions relating to *Patterns of Continuity and Change over Time*, you could use the matrix to identify additional lessons that test that specific historical skill.

By completing these tasks, you will develop both the factual foundation and the reasoning skills necessary to become more proficient at thinking historically.

Worksheets for Primary Sources

To help you with the difficult task of document analysis, a set of **worksheets** has been provided in Appendix C. You can use these as a starting point for your analysis of primary sources.

All sources are not created equal, so use the worksheet that is appropriate for each source, e.g., document excerpts, visual sources, and maps. While the worksheets might seem simplistic, they will help you to organize your ideas so that you can more easily make complex connections.

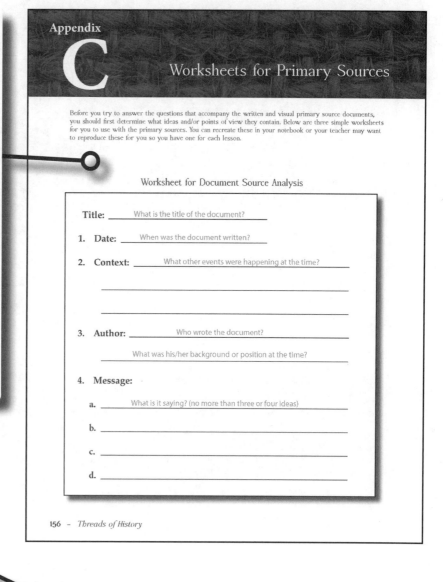

Some of the lessons contain icons to remind you to utilize the primary source worksheets.

Threads Walk-Through

The Mini-Reader

Appendix D — The Mini-Reader

Threads of History provides not only thematic content review, but also serves as a small book of readings and visual sources to accompany your textbook and class notes. It's like two for the price of one! The following is a chronological list of the primary source documents available in this edition of *Threads*:

Year	Page	Type	Topic	Year	Page	Type	Topic
1649	12		Puritan Church Platform to the General Court of Massachusetts	1841	82		Constitution of Brook Farm
1776	26		Loyalist view of the American Revolution	1845	69		John O'Sullivan and Manifest Destiny
1786	8		George Washington on Shays' Rebellion	1850	56		John C. Calhoun and the Compromise of 1850
1801	18		Thomas Jefferson's First Inaugural Address	1851	22		The Second Great Awakening
1811	52		Felix Grundy and the causes of the War of 1812	1853	68		Expansion of the United States, 1783–1853
1823	60		Reaction of *McCulloch v. Maryland*	1867	98		Thaddeus Stevens and Reconstruction
1823	146		Monroe Doctrine	1868	78		The Fourteenth Amendment
1825	43		John Quincy Adams and the role of government	1873	48		The Granger Movement
1832	30		Andrew Jackson's veto of the National Bank	1876	4		The Election of 1876
1833	86		William Lloyd Garrison and Abolition	1883	102		U.S. Civil Rights Cases
				1883	110		William Graham Sumner on Social Darwinism

160 - *Threads of History*

Practice with primary sources is invaluable in your preparations for the exam. As such, a list of the historical sources included throughout this edition of *Threads* has been included in Appendix D. Here you can easily find and integrate specific primary sources into your study plans. Working with primary sources not only prepares you for the exam, but for college, career, and even independent research!

A couple of last thoughts as you meet the challenge of AP United States history and begin using *Threads of History* in your AP class. The materials in the book are based on a fundamental principle: *there is no magic bullet or quick, easy road to success on the AP United States History examination.* Nothing can replace competent classroom instruction and dedicated study. It is only through a daily effort in building your knowledge and improving your thinking and writing skills that you are likely to qualify for college credit and/or placement on the AP test. You must pay close attention to all classroom activities, complete all assignments, and **read your textbook carefully!** All this said, I hope that *Threads of History* is a valuable tool in helping you master the AP curriculum this year, and that you have a successful and rich experience in your class culminating with a 5 on the exam in May.

Michael Henry

Review & Source Activities

Lesson 1

Historical Periods

By the time you are ready to take the Advanced Placement (AP) test in May, you will have been bombarded by hundreds of facts and dates. In this blizzard of information, it is possible to lose track of the broad delineations of U.S. history. On the AP test, however, there will often be essay questions or multiple-choice questions that refer to a historical period rather than to a set of specific years. Unless you are familiar with the labels for these eras, you may misinterpret or incorrectly answer parts a question that you could otherwise easily master.

The following chart presents the major historical periods of U.S. history. In addition, it identifies events that roughly marked the beginning and ending of the era. You might review the chart by looking at a list of events (perhaps in the index of your primary textbook) and placing them in their appropriate historical period. This will help you develop a stronger chronological sense and decrease the likelihood of encountering unfamiliar time references on the AP test.

Directions: Analyze the chart on historical periods, and then answer the following questions.

1. Which one of the following events did NOT occur during the antebellum period?
   - (A) the ratification of the Fourteenth Amendment
   - (B) the development of the cotton gin
   - (C) the dispute over slavery in Missouri
   - (D) the dispute over the tariff in South Carolina

2. Federal government regulation of the meat industry and the beginnings of the Great War (World War I) occurred during
   - (A) the Gilded Age
   - (B) the Progressive Era
   - (C) the New Deal Era
   - (D) the Fair Deal Era

3. Which one of the following events occurred during the Gilded Age?
   - (A) the end of the War of 1812
   - (B) the election of Andrew Jackson as president
   - (C) the end of World War II
   - (D) the election of Ulysses Grant as president

Major Historical Periods throughout U.S. History

Period	Date	Events marking beginnings and endings
Colonial Period	1607–1763	1. Jamestown founded 2. French and Indian War ended
Revolutionary Period	1763–1783	1. England ended salutary neglect 2. Treaty of Paris signed ending Revolution
Confederation Period	1781–1789	1. States surrender their western land claims 2. Constitution ratified
Era of Good Feelings	1815–1824	1. War of 1812 ended 2. Election of 1824
Jacksonian Era	1828–1848	1. Andrew Jackson elected president 2. Mexican War ended/James Polk leaves office
Antebellum Period (South before Civil War)	1793–1861	1. Cotton gin invented/rise of slavery 2. Civil War started
Reconstruction Era	1865–1877	1. Civil War ended 2. Compromise of 1877
Gilded Age	1868–1901	1. Ulysses Grant elected president 2. Assassination of William McKinley
Progressive Era	1901–1917	1. Square Deal began 2. America entered the Great War
New Deal Era	1933–1939	1. Franklin Roosevelt began his presidency 2. World War II began in Europe
Fair Deal Era	1945–1953	1. Truman became president/F.D.R. died 2. Korean War divided nation/Truman retired
New Frontier/ Great Society Era	1961–1968	1. John Kennedy became president 2. Vietnam War divided nation

Lesson 1: Historical Periods

Source Activities

Directions: Using the map below and your knowledge of American history, answer the following questions.

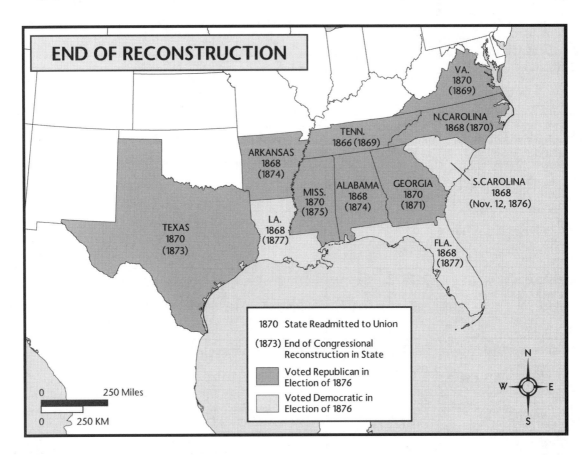

Multiple-Choice

1. The map best serves as evidence of which of the following?

   (A) that the Civil War resentments had been forgotten
   (B) that the Radical Republicans' plan for equality was in retreat
   (C) that the Republican Party had made lasting gains in the South
   (D) that a "Solid South" had formed in the former Confederacy

2. What Republican Party decision in 1876–1877 marked the end of Reconstruction?

   (A) the withdrawal of military support from several Reconstruction governments in the South
   (B) the suspension of tariff duties collection in the South for ten years
   (C) the exemption of several Southern states from enforcing the Fourteenth Amendment
   (D) the concession of the presidential election to the Democrats

Short-Answer

Using the map, answer parts a, b, and c.

a) Historians often mark the election of 1876 as a turning point in the history of Reconstruction. Choose ONE of the groups below and explain how their lives were most changed by the results of the election and cite ONE piece of evidence to support your choice:
- Freedmen
- Redeemers
- Radical Republicans

b) Contrast your choice with ONE of the other options above and explain why your selected group experienced the greater transformation in their lives.

c) Briefly explain ONE other event from 1876–1896 that marked a departure from Reconstruction Era ideals.

Lesson 2

Famous Rebellions

Several armed rebellions helped shape American development before the Civil War. Three early uprisings (Bacon's, Shays', and Whiskey Rebellions) were sparked by economic and political grievances against authority that was perceived as arbitrary and distant. Each of the clashes played a transformational role in its era: Bacon's Rebellion helped weaken the indentured servant system; Shays' Rebellion undermined the already dwindling support for the Articles of Confederation; and the Whiskey Rebellion established the authority of the new national government and moved George Washington firmly into the Federalist Party camp. The chart on the next page will help you analyze these rebellions.

As you consider the chart, you may wish to evaluate whether these early dissenters were driven by their inherently rebellious nature, the rugged frontier environment, unfair government actions, or a combination of all these factors.

Nat Turner's revolt differed significantly from the previous rebellions. It epitomized the great nightmare of the antebellum slavocracy—a large-scale slave revolt. The uprising stands alone as the most dramatic and violent slave revolt in U.S. history. The Turner Rebellion also reinforced the South's commitment to slavery and made peaceful manumission almost impossible. Historians have speculated about why there were no other major slave uprisings. How would you explain this lack of large-scale slave resistance?

Directions: Analyze the chart on famous rebellions, and then answer the following questions.

1. The most significant result of Nat Turner's rebellion was
   (A) the South's intensified commitment to slavery
   (B) Abraham Lincoln's decision to emancipate the slaves
   (C) the formation of the American Colonization Society
   (D) the emancipation of most of the slaves in Virginia

2. Which of the following individuals would favor the actions taken by the national government during the Whiskey Rebellion?
   (A) a backcountry farmer who supported the Articles of Confederation
   (B) a states' rights supporter who feared a strong central government
   (C) a Quaker who opposed the use of force
   (D) a supporter of law and order

3. The common element of Bacon's, Shays', and the Whiskey Rebellion was that
   (A) all resulted in changes in the economic conditions that caused them
   (B) all occurred before the American Revolution
   (C) all were challenges to perceived unfairness by a distant government
   (D) all resulted in widespread changes in American society

Three Major Rebellions in Early U.S. History

	Date	Cause	Events	Significance
Nathaniel Bacon's Rebellion	1676	Virginia frontiersmen seeking land clashed with Indians Frontiersmen demanded help from government Jamestown refused aid, fearing Indian War	Bacon and his men lived on frontier Bacon and his men stormed Jamestown Burned Jamestown Bacon died of fever Rebellion collapsed	Colonial rebellion against government authority Clash between east/west, rich/poor Tidewater's discrimination against frontiersmen *Revision of indentured servant system, greater reliance on slave labor*
Daniel Shays' Rebellion	1786–1787	Unfair taxes in Massachusetts Farms foreclosed Farmers imprisoned as debtors	Shays/1,200 men attacked courts in western Massachusetts State militia put down rebellion	Uprising was a general threat to property Threat that rebellion could spread to other states *Articles of Confederation viewed as too weak to maintain law and order* Bolstered call for revisions of Articles (Constitutional Convention, 1787)
Whiskey Rebellion	1794–1795	Farmers in western Pennsylvania refused to pay federal excise tax on whiskey Attacked tax collectors Farmers compared tax to Stamp Act of 1765	Washington called for 13,000 troops to suppress the rebels Rebels dispersed, ceased rebellion	Put the force of the government behind the Constitution Government could *and would* enforce the law /constitution Constitution protected law/order Hamilton's idea of an energetic national government prevailed
Nat Turner's (slave) Rebellion	1831	Slaves wanted freedom Nat Turner saw "vision" and attacked whites in Southampton County, Virginia	Turner, 70 slaves, and 55 whites killed Turner caught; he was executed, and hundreds of slaves were punished	Frightened South Tightened slave codes Restricted freedom for all blacks in South South began to aggressively defend slavery as a "positive good"

Source Activities

Directions: Using the excerpt below and your knowledge of American history, answer the following questions.

> "Without an alteration in our political creed, the superstructure we have been seven years in raising at the expense of so much treasure and blood, must fall. We are fast verging to anarchy and confusion…What stronger evidence can be given of the want of energy in our government, than these disorders?…Thirteen sovereignties pulling against each other, and all tugging at the federal head, will soon bring ruin on the whole…"
>
> —Letter from George Washington to James Madison, November 5, 1786

Multiple-Choice

1. Which of the following alterations in America's political creed would George Washington most likely support?

    (A) revising the governing principles of the American Revolution

    (B) promoting debt relief and currency reform

    (C) encouraging greater regional cooperation and trade

    (D) aligning America's creed more closely to that of Great Britain

2. The sentiments expressed in the letter led most directly to late eighteenth-century political controversies over the issue of the

    (A) creation of the National Bank

    (B) ratification of the Jay Treaty

    (C) establishment of a presidential Cabinet

    (D) collection of excise taxes on whiskey

8 - *Threads of History*

Short-Answer

Using the excerpt, answer parts a and b.

a) Shays' Rebellion affected Washington's political thinking. Briefly explain how the disorder changed Washington's position on TWO of the following:
- Suppression of dissent in the mid-1780s
- The effectiveness of the Articles of Confederation
- Attendance at the Philadelphia meeting to amend the Articles of Confederation

b) Briefly explain how ONE of Washington's positions expressed in <u>part a</u> could be challenged in the mid- and late 1780s.

Lesson 2: Famous Rebellions - 9

Lesson 3

Religious Development, 1619-1740

Religion played an important role in the founding and development of the British colonies in North America. The English Reformation generated alienation and turmoil for many religious denominations in Great Britain. Catholics were upset when Henry VIII created the Anglican Church and displaced the Pope as the religious leader of England. Other groups such as the Congregational Church (Puritans) and the Society of Friends (Quakers) challenged the beliefs and powers exercised by the new state-sponsored church. These groups began to look to North America as a place to realize their dreams of religious freedom.

These dissenters founded several colonies in the New World. For example, in New England, the Puritans settled Massachusetts Bay in hopes of purifying their church. In Maryland, the Catholics sought a place of unfettered worship, and, in Pennsylvania, the Quakers hoped to find religious freedom and noninterference.

Most historians agree that religious freedom and tolerance were stronger in the British colonies than in the mother country. As you study the chart, consider what factors contributed to this freedom. Where was religious tolerance least likely to occur in the colonies during the seventeenth century?

Directions: Analyze the chart on religious development, and then answer the following questions.

1. Which area of the British colonies maintained state-supported, religious practices similar to those found in the mother country?
   (A) Massachusetts and Connecticut
   (B) Virginia and Maryland
   (C) the frontiers of Georgia and South Carolina
   (D) Pennsylvania and New York

2. Which religious group faced the greatest persecution in the colonies?
   (A) Congregational Church
   (B) Presbyterian Church
   (C) Society of Friends
   (D) Catholic Church

3. Which of the following groups was characterized by beliefs in innate depravity, predestination, and intolerance of other religions?
   (A) Anglicans
   (B) Catholics
   (C) Quakers
   (D) Puritans

Religious Development in the Colonies

	Congregational Church (Puritans)	Anglican Church	Society of Friends (Quakers)	Catholic Church	Presbyterian Church
Leaders	John Cotton John Winthrop Cotton Mather	King or queen of England Bishop of London	George Fox William Penn	Pope in Rome Bishops Priests	Francis Makemie William Tennent
Areas of Influence	New England	Virginia Maryland	Pennsylvania Scattered in New England, New Jersey	Maryland (early) Scattered in parts of Pennsylvania	Frontier and backcountry; Pennsylvania, New Jersey
Beliefs	Man is depraved/sinful One is saved or damned at birth Wicked life was a sign of damnation Only "visible saints" were saved Intolerant of all other religions Coerced nonbelievers with force or banishment	King/queen headed church King's power came from God Used Book of Common Prayer Some Catholic liturgy and doctrine maintained	"Inner light" a guide to salvation Minimal church structure All people equal in God's eyes Pacifism Refused to take oaths Tolerant of other religions	Strict hierarchy with Pope at head Salvation earned by good works, faith, loyalty to church Priests were path to God No divorce allowed	Calvinism Split from Puritans over church governance Power lay with church elders Like other Protestants, accepted Jesus as savior Tolerant of other religions
Comment	By 1740 church represented largest denomination in colonies Lost much of their poltical influence in New England after 1700 Intolerance cost its support Hoped to create a religious "City Upon a Hill"	By 1740 had second-largest membership in colonies Much less influence in colonies than in England Being a member carried great status in colonies	Grew from Puritanism Clashed often with Puritans "Holy Experiment" in Pennsylvania	Maryland originally a Catholic haven Catholics very unpopular in other colonies, where they could not vote or hold office	By 1740 had third-largest membership in colonies Scotch/Irish immigrants changed church in early 1700s Split between New/Old Lights

Lesson 3: Religious Development, 1619–1740

Source Activities

Directions: Using the excerpt below and your knowledge of American history, answer the following questions.

> "(1) The doors of the churches of Christ upon earth do not by God's appointment stand so wide open, that all sorts of people, good and bad, may freely enter therein at their pleasure, but such as are admitted thereto, as members, ought to be examined and tried first, whether they fit and meet to be received into church-society or not...
>
> (6) ...The end of the magistrate's office is not only the quiet and peaceable life of the subject in matters of righteousness and honesty, but also in matters of godliness; yea, of all godliness...profanation of the Lord's Day,...disturbing the peaceable administration and exercise of the worship and holy things of God...and the like...are to be restrained and punished by civil authority."
>
> —Platform of Church Discipline adopted by the General Court of Massachusetts, 1649

Multiple-Choice

1. The authors of the Platform of Church Discipline would most likely oppose which of the following ideas?

   (A) punishment of religious dissenters
   (B) holding church services during periods of unrest
   (C) separating church and government functions
   (D) restricting church membership to a select few

2. In creating the new nation in the 1780s and 1790s, the Founding Fathers challenged the main idea of the passage above by prohibiting

   (A) regional church control of their membership
   (B) government establishment and support of churches
   (C) church members from serving in government
   (D) private cash donations to churches

Short Answer

Using the excerpt, answer parts a, b, and c.

a) Briefly explain the main points made in the Platform of Church Discipline.

b) Briefly explain why the Massachusetts Court adopted the measures expressed in the excerpt.

c) Briefly explain how the ideas expressed in the passage helped form a distinct New England identity from 1620–1660.

you can associate major events, such as wars, depressions, and land acquisitions, with various presidents. As you study the presidential charts, also consider why there were periods of undistinguished presidents. The two eras of forgotten presidents were 1837–1861 and 1865–1901. Why do you think these two periods were characterized by presidential mediocrity?

The first chart summarizes the achievements of our four greatest presidents. In all cases, these leaders achieved major domestic successes and/or promoted America's strength and security in foreign relations. In addition, each man changed American political thinking and transformed the office of president. Historians suggest that, in order to achieve presidential greatness, a president must make the office "a more splendid instrument of democracy." What do you think this means? Do you feel any other presidents deserve the label of greatness? Why?

Directions: Analyze the charts on the presidents, and then answer the following questions.

1. Between 1861 and 1889, a common element among the presidential administrations was that most presidents

   (A) were impeached
   (B) were from the Democratic Party
   (C) were from the Republican Party
   (D) had personal scandals in their administrations

2. What common characteristic did the presidencies of Ulysses Grant, Warren Harding, and Richard Nixon have?

   (A) All had scandals during their administrations.
   (B) All were Democratic administrations.
   (C) All had wars begin during their administrations.
   (D) All were famous generals.

3. What characteristic did the great presidents of the United States share?

   (A) Each survived a political scandal during his presidency.
   (B) Each won a foreign war during his presidency.
   (C) Each dealt with an economic depression during his presidency.
   (D) Each had a major legislative success during his presidency.

The Four Greatest Presidents

President	Domestic Success	Foreign Success	Lasting Impact on Country/Presidency
George Washington	Bill of Rights approved National Bank founded Established authority of federal government to tax citizens Government authority established by Whiskey Rebellion	Jay Treaty: British out of forts in Northwest Maintained neutrality in European war Farewell Address advocated no entangling alliances Treaty of San Lorenzo with Spain opened up the Mississippi River to American trade	Created/established dignity and power of president Sound financial footing established Isolationism toward Europe proposed Secured the "West" (area beyond the Appalachian Mountains)
Thomas Jefferson	Reduced size of government Abolished Whiskey Tax Reduced national debt Pardoned Sedition Act violators Enacted Judiciary Act to reform court system	Negotiated Louisiana Purchase Barbary pirate wars establish respect for U.S. Kept U.S. out of European war	Achieved peaceful transition of power between parties Doubled geographic size of U.S. Promoted rights rather than control of people by government
Abraham Lincoln	Preserved the Union Emancipation Proclamation and Thirteenth Amendment Passed the Homestead Act Reformed banking system	Kept Europe out of Civil War	Kept nation whole Gave nation a new birth of freedom Expanded president's war-making power
Franklin Roosevelt	Created New Deal reforms to combat Depression Established Social Security Assisted homeless and unemployed Federal Deposit Insurance Corp. established Security and Exchange Commission created Civil Conservation Corp. founded	Led U.S. through World War II Established United Nations Led U.S. from isolationism to internationalism	America became a superpower Government permanently expanded its role in society Focused attention and power in Oval Office

Lesson 4: Presidents of the United States

All Presidents with Adminstration Highlights

President	Term	Party	Major Events/Developments
George Washington	1789–1797	Federalist	Establishes new government; Whiskey Rebellion; Jay Treaty; Farewell Address
John Adams	1797–1801	Federalist	Undeclared war with France (Quasi War); XYZ affair; Alien and Sedition Acts
Thomas Jefferson	1801–1809	(Democratic) Republican	First Republican president; Executed Louisiana Purchase; Embargo Act of 1807
James Madison	1809–1817	(Democratic) Republican	War of 1812
James Monroe	1817–1825	(Democratic) Republican	Florida purchase; Era of Good Feelings; Executed the Missouri Compromise and the Monroe Doctrine
John Q. Adams	1825–1829	(National) Republican	Corrupt bargain
Andrew Jackson	1829–1837	Democrat	Expands presidential power; Bank battle; Tariff/Nullification Crisis; Indian removal
Martin Van Buren	1837–1841	Democrat	Panic of 1837; Trail of Tears
William H. Harrison	1841–1841	Whig	First Whig president; Died in office
John Tyler	1841–1845	Whig	Annexation of Texas
James K. Polk	1845–1849	Democrat	Mexican-American War; Mexican Cession
Zachary Taylor	1849–1850	Whig	Last Whig president elected; Died in office
Millard Fillmore	1850–1853	Whig	Compromise of 1850
Franklin Pierce	1853–1857	Democrat	Kansas-Nebraska Act; Ostend Manifesto
James Buchanan	1857–1861	Democrat	Dred Scott decision; John Brown's raid; Seven states leave Union
Abraham Lincoln	1861–1865	Republican	Civil War; Emancipation Proclamation; First president assassinated
Andrew Johnson	1865–1869	Republican	Reconstruction; First president impeached; Purchased Alaska
Ulysses S. Grant	1869–1877	Republican	Reconstruction continued; Many scandals
Rutherford B. Hayes	1877–1881	Republican	Compromise of 1877; Reconstruction ended
James Garfield	1881–1881	Republican	Second president assassinated
Chester Arthur	1881–1885	Republican	Pendleton Act

All Presidents with Adminstration Highlights

President	Term	Party	Major Events/Developments
Grover Cleveland	1885–1889	Democrat	First Democratic president since Civil War; Tariff battle with Congress
Benjamin Harrison	1889–1893	Republican	Built up navy; Grandson of William H. Harrison; McKinley Tariff
Grover Cleveland	1893–1897	Democrat	Only president to serve two nonconsecutive terms; Depression of 1893
William McKinley	1897–1901	Republican	Spanish-American War; (imperialism) Third president assassinated
Theodore Roosevelt	1901–1909	Republican	Trust buster; Square Deal reforms; "Big stick" in Caribbean
William Howard Taft	1909–1913	Republican	Dollar Diplomacy in Caribbean; Split with Theodore Roosevelt in 1912
Woodrow Wilson	1913–1921	Democrat	New Freedom Progressive reforms; World War I; Fought for League of Nations
Warren Harding	1921–1923	Republican	Normalcy period; Political and personal scandals; Died in office [Teapot Dome scandal]
Calvin Coolidge	1923–1929	Republican	Pro-business, *laissez-faire* administration; Kellogg-Briand Pact (outlaws aggressive war)
Herbert Hoover	1929–1933	Republican	Great Depression strikes; Promoted attitude of rugged individualism
Franklin D. Roosevelt	1933–1945	Democrat	New Deal reforms; World War II; Elected to four terms
Harry S. Truman	1945–1953	Democrat	Fair Deal reforms; Cold War begins; Upset victory in 1948; Korean War
Dwight Eisenhower	1953–1961	Republican	Ended Korean War; Maintained peaceful coexistence with USSR; Established modern Republicanism
John F. Kennedy	1961–1963	Democrat	New Frontier reforms; Bay of Pigs; Cuban Missile Crisis; Assassinated 1963
Lyndon B. Johnson	1963–1969	Democrat	Great Society reforms; Civil rights acts; Escalated Vietnam War
Richard Nixon	1969–1974	Republican	Ended Vietnam War; Recognized China; Watergate scandal; First president to resign
Gerald Ford	1974–1977	Republican	Took over when Nixon resigned; Pardoned Nixon for his crimes
Jimmy Carter	1977–1981	Democrat	Camp David Accords; Iran Hostage Crisis
Ronald Reagan	1981–1989	Republican	Supply-side economics; Military buildup; Soviet Union's Cold War decline began
George H. W. Bush	1989-1993	Republican	Collapse of Soviet Union; End of Cold War; First Gulf War
William (Bill) Clinton	1993-2001	Democrat	Dismantling of Soviet Empire; Welfare Reform; Impeachment

Source Activities

Directions: Using the excerpt below and your knowledge of American history, answer the following questions.

> "...this [election] being now decided by the voice of the nation, announced according to the rules of the Constitution, all will, of course, arrange themselves under the will of the law, and unite in common efforts for the common good. All, too, will bear in mind this sacred principle, that through the will of the majority is in all cases to prevail, that will to be rightful must be reasonable; that the minority possess their equal rights, which equal law must protect, and to violate would be oppression...
>
> We are all Republicans, we are all Federalists. If there be any among us who would wish to dissolve this Union or to change its republican form, let them stand undisturbed as monuments of the safety with which error of opinion may be tolerated where reason is left free to combat it..."
>
> —Thomas Jefferson, March 4, 1801

Multiple-Choice

1. Based on Jefferson's speech of 1801, which one of the following governmental actions would he most likely support?
   - (A) accepting peaceful disunion
   - (B) suppressing dangerous dissent
   - (C) establishing bi-partisan relationships
   - (D) modifying the system of federalism

2. The passage above was likely written in response to the earlier government attempts to
   - (A) add new territories without congressional approval
   - (B) limit political freedoms of expression and dissent
   - (C) enhance the power of the president through the veto
   - (D) alter international trade policies by treaties

Short-Answer

Using the excerpt, answer parts a, b, and c.

a) Identify the main points Thomas Jefferson outlined in his 1801 speech.

b) Briefly explain ONE action taken by President Jefferson that challenged the sentiment expressed in the excerpt.

c) Briefly discuss how ONE of these ideas was most important in explaining why historians ranked Jefferson as a great president.

Lesson 5

The First and Second Great Awakenings

American history has been marked by several religious, often evangelical, upheavals. Two of the most significant occurred in the mid-eighteenth and nineteenth centuries and were known as the First and Second Great Awakening. Neither developed as a tightly coordinated movement. Rather, these revivals were a series of local events linked together by "a religion of the heart." Both challenged their congregations to renounce sin, seek salvation, and reform their daily lives.

The First Great Awakening began in England and spread to the American colonies in the 1730s and 1740s. It presented a Calvinistic message of predestination, original sin, and a punishing God. The Second Great Awakening began in the 1790s on the American frontier and spread into New England and New York in the 1830s and 1840s. It attacked sinfulness, secularism (materialism), and offered salvation for both individuals and society. Although each movement presented unique messages, they both transformed the social, political, and religious thinking of their eras.

The chart on the following page compares and contrasts the two Awakenings. As you study it, think about the conditions that existed in mid-eighteenth and nineteenth century America that gave rise to these two revivals. In addition, contrast each movement's message, its approach to salvation, and how each transformed people's attitudes about themselves and society.

Directions: Analyze the chart on the two Great Awakenings, and then answer the following questions.

1. Both the First and Second Great Awakening
   (A) presented a Calvinistic message of salvation
   (B) called for the abolition of slavery
   (C) appealed to many classes/levels of society
   (D) offered a less emotional form of worship

2. The First Great Awakening promoted which of the following ideas:
   (A) salvation at birth through God's grace
   (B) social reform before personal salvation
   (C) allowing only ordained, trained ministers to preach
   (D) political revolt against British rule

3. Members of both Awakenings would agree with which of the following statements?
   (A) "The world is too much with us… Getting and spending we lay waste our powers."
   (B) "Women are equal to men in both intellectual and moral attributes."
   (C) "Slavery must be abolished immediately without compensation."
   (D) "Man is always better whipped than damned."

The Great Awakenings

	First Great Awakening	Second Great Awakening
Background/ Causes	Began in England with John Wesley's, and George Whitefield's crusades Rise in secularism Met outdoors; often involved 1,000s Countered Enlightenment's rationalism Whitefield brought ideas to colonies	Rise in secularism Desire to strengthen public morality Met outdoors; often involved 1,000s Grew from "camp meetings" of 1790s (Cane Ridge, Kentucky) spread to "burned-over district" of New York
Participants	Lower classes: laborers, servants, small farmers Many women converts; free/enslaved blacks Many church dominations, but Baptists, Methodists, Presbyterians in forefront	Many women converts Evangelical Baptists, Methodists, Presbyterians in forefront Millennialists: second coming of Christ Some African Americans, Native Americans Reform groups: temperance, abolitionists
Ideas	Predestination: salvation by faith/grace not by good works (Calvinistic) Stressed universality of sin Repent sins; reaffirm faith Choose Christ or Hell Literal interpretation of Bible	Rejected Calvinism: salvation through good works/personal efforts Believed people are "free moral agents" Universal salvation Belief in personal/societal perfection Condemned greed/indifference to poor
Leaders	George Whitefield-main spokesman; emotional/spoke to throngs outdoors Jonathan Edwards: "Sinners in the Hands of an Angry God." William/Gilbert Tennent- Presbyterian ministers Theodore Frelinghuysen- Dutch Reform minister	Charles Grandison Finney-evangelical minister in the "burned-over district" James McGready-Presbyterian leader of camp meetings Peter Cartwright-Methodist circuit rider Timothy Dwight-spread ideas at Yale college and in New England
Impact	Challenged clergy: untutored ministers could preach Attacked status quo: egalitarian with universal salvation; challenged deference Spoke out against slaves' treatment, but did not support abolition of slavery Divided churches: "Old Light" / "New Light" Presbyterians; turmoil in Congregational and Dutch Reform churches as well Promoted inter-colonial communication and cooperation	Energized reformers: abolition, temperance, peace movement, women's rights Promoted personal self improvement Individual could remake self and society Divided social classes/churches Increased membership in evangelical churches (Methodists/ Baptists) Rise of more emotional, personal approach to God and salvation

Source Activities

Directions: Using the illustration below and your knowledge of American history, answer the following questions.

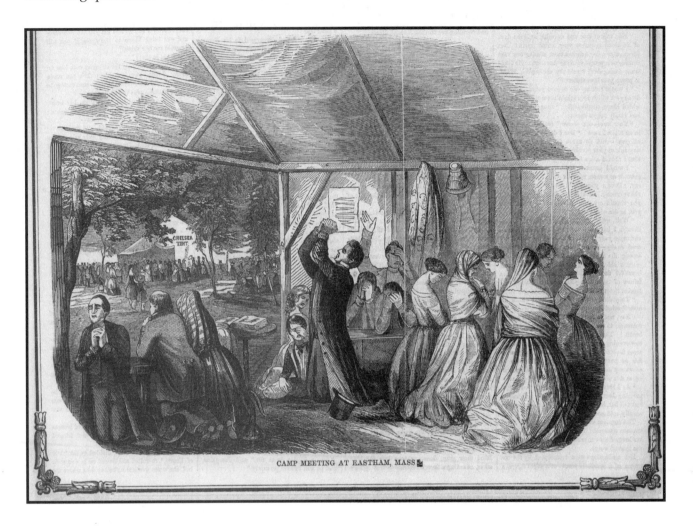
CAMP MEETING AT EASTHAM, MASS.

Multiple-Choice

1. Which of the following twentieth-century continuities most closely parallels the developments during the Second Great Awakening?

    (A) religious groups' support of "Born-Again Christians" in political races

    (B) religious groups' defense of creationism in the schools

    (C) religious groups' promotion of social and economic changes in society

    (D) religious groups' crusade for universal peace

2. Which of the following activities highlighted in the illustration made the Second Great Awakening controversial before the Civil War?

    (A) the movement's call for an end to slavery

    (B) the movement's rejection of the idea of progress in society

    (C) the movement's involvement of clergy in political reform

    (D) the movement's involvement of women in changing society

22 - *Threads of History*

Short-Answer

Using the illustration, answer parts a, b, and c.

a) Briefly explain how the principles of the Second Great Awakening transformed the group identity of ONE of the following:
- Women participants in the Great Awakening
- Clergy in the Great Awakening
- Male participants in the Great Awakening

b) Briefly explain how ONE development from 1820–1840 promoted the point of view expressed in the picture.

c) Briefly explain how ONE development from 1820–1840 challenged the point of view in the picture.

Lesson

Coming of the American Revolution

Although the first shots of the American Revolution were fired in 1775, trouble between England and its colonies had been building for many years. During the 1740s, European conflicts spilled into the colonies, creating continuous trouble over issues of economic, military, and political sovereignty. Some historians believe that the British policy of "salutary neglect" ended as early as 1748, at the conclusion of King George's War. Others suggest it didn't end until 1763, when British policy toward the colonies changed drastically following the French and Indian War. At that time, England sought to raise revenue in America to pay down its national debt and to provide for colonial defenses. Britain proposed to do this through a series of revenue acts and policies designed to tighten its system of mercantilism.

The chart on the next page traces the British attempt to bring the American colonies closer to the empire after 1763. As you study it, consider whether, given the British mercantilist system and the colonial mind-set of the 1760s and 1770s, the American Revolution could have been avoided.

Directions: Analyze the chart on the acts and reactions leading up to the American Revolution, and then answer the following questions.

1. From 1764 to 1773, the principal British method of raising revenue in the colonies was to
   (A) tax the trade and commerce of the colonies
   (B) tax the income of individual colonists
   (C) permit colonial legislatures to raise money for their own needs
   (D) sell land in the West

2. What was the colonists' most common method of protesting British taxation policy from 1764 to 1773?
   (A) to complain but to pay the taxes
   (B) to offer Britain an alternative means of raising revenue
   (C) to refuse to import or use British products/goods
   (D) to deal with Britain on a colony-by-colony basis

3. The most common British reaction to colonial resistance from 1764 to 1773 was to pass a tax or take an action, experience colonial resistance, and then
   (A) strongly confront the colonials
   (B) back away from the tax or action
   (C) appeal to the churches for help with enforcement
   (D) use foreign troops to overcome it

24 - *Threads of History*

Acts, Actions, and Reactions Leading Up to American Revolution

Act or Action	Purpose	Provisions of Act	Colonial Reaction	British Reaction
Proclamation Line of 1763	British hoped to pacify Indians in West Pacification would reduce need for troops to battle Indians on frontier	Forbade settlement west of Appalachian Mountains Everyone in the western region must return to the East	Anger; colonists had fought French and Indian War to gain access to western region Colonists continued to settle in the area	British modified law with Treaty of Fort Stanwix, 1768 Moved line of permitted settlement farther to west
Sugar Act 1764	Act passed to raise money for colonial defense	Duty on foreign molasses had been reduced but now would be enforced	Anger Smuggling	Attempted to enforce tax
Stamp Act 1765	Passed to raise money Same tax existed in Great Britain	Taxed dice, playing cards, newspapers, marriage licenses Total of 50 items taxed	Convened Stamp Act Congress Petitioned the King Urban riots Boycotted goods Viewed as an internal tax	Repealed law Little money raised
Declaratory Act 1766	When Stamp Act repealed, British needed to save face	England could pass any laws for the colonies	Ignored it	British attempt to assert their dwindling authority
Townshend Act 1767	Passed to raise money and regulate trade External tax	Taxed imports: glass, paint, lead, paper, tea	Boycott of British goods Urban riots	Repealed taxes on everything but tea in 1770
Boston Massacre 1770	British troops in city to enforce laws	n/a	Confronted soldiers	Opened fire on mob, five colonists killed
Boston Tea Party 1773	Colonists protested tea tax	Tax on tea from 1770 remained	Sons of Liberty threw 342 cases of tea into Boston Harbor	Intolerable or Coercive Acts passed
First Continental Congress 1774	Met to decide how to help Massachusetts resist Intolerable Acts	n/a	Pled to King to repeal the Intolerable Acts Boycotted taxed goods Called another Congress in 1775	Put troops in cities Decided to hold firm

Lesson 6: Coming of the American Revolution

Source Activities

Directions: Using the excerpt below and your knowledge of American history, answer the following questions.

> "Suppose we were to revolt from Great Britain, declare ourselves independent, and set up a Republic of our own—what would be the consequences? —I stand aghast at the prospect—my blood runs chill while I think of the calamities, the complicated evils that must follow…
>
> What a horrid situation would thousands be reduced to who have taken the oath of allegiance to the King. They must renounce that allegiance, or abandon all their property in America! By a Declaration of Independency, every avenue to a compromise with Great Britain would be closed. The sword only could decide the quarrel…
>
> Devastation and ruin must mark the progress of this war along the sea coast of America. …But supposing once more that we were able to cut off every regiment that Britain can spare or hire, and to destroy every ship she can send. Suppose we could beat off any other European power that would presume to invade this continent. Yet, a republican form of government would neither suit the spirit of the people, nor the size of America."
>
> —Charles Inglis, "The True Interest of America Impartially Stated," 1776

Multiple-Choice

1. Which of the following groups would most directly challenge the ideas expressed in "The True Interest of America Impartially Stated?"

   (A) ministers of King George in the southern colonies
   (B) members of the Free African Society
   (C) merchants with trade relations with Great Britain
   (D) members of the Sons of Liberty

2. Which of the following controversies after the American Revolution most directly developed from the clash of national identity suggested in the excerpt above?

   (A) disputes over compensation for confiscated property
   (B) disputes over Native American land claims
   (C) disputes over ending the slave trade
   (D) disputes over trade relations with Great Britain

6

Short-Answer

Using the excerpt, answer parts a, b, and c.

a) From 1765–1776, a new American identity emerged in the British colonies. Select ONE of the events below and briefly explain how it contributed to this emerging national identity:
- The Stamp Act Congress (1765)
- The Boston Massacre (1770)
- The Boston Tea Party (1773)

b) Briefly analyze ONE other element of the emerging American identity that was not discussed in part a.

c) Briefly explain ONE attempt by the British government to suppress the emerging American identity from 1765–1776.

Lesson 7

The National Banks

The National Banks of the United States dominated American economic history from 1791 to 1845. No issue was more contentious between Federalists and Republicans as these two parties established the financial foundation of the nation. In the early years of the Republic, Alexander Hamilton's supporters clashed with Thomas Jefferson's supporters over the Bank's constitutionality and its alleged unfairness to the poor.

Later, the rechartering of the Bank sparked a raging controversy between the Jacksonian Democrats and Henry Clay's Whigs. Further, it divided the country geographically as western farmers blamed the Bank for their economic woes and saw it as a symbol of eastern financial elitism and dominance.

The following chart summarizes the First and Second Banks of the United States. It can be used in conjunction with the chart on political parties (Lesson 10). As you study the Bank, consider why it was so controversial. Can you think of any other economic issue that so dominated United States history?

Directions: Analyze the chart on the National Banks, and then answer the following questions.

1. A primary reason for opposition to the National Banks was that these banks

    (A) failed to provide sound economic services to the country

    (B) contributed to foreign speculation in the American economy

    (C) promoted speculation and risk-taking in banking

    (D) were not authorized by the Constitution

2. The person most likely to support the First National Bank would be someone who

    (A) farmed in the frontier regions of Tennessee

    (B) voted for Thomas Jefferson in the presidential election of 1796

    (C) lived in Philadelphia and was involved in commerce and trade

    (D) feared the rapid expansion of government power in the 1790s

3. The main argument for rechartering the National Bank in 1816 was that

    (A) England had a national bank and America must remain competitive

    (B) the Bank would prevent falling land prices from hurting economic growth

    (C) the Constitution had been amended and Congress now had the power to create a Bank

    (D) the Bank could restore economic stability after the War of 1812

The National Banks

	First Bank	Second Bank
Years	1791–1811	1816–1836
Reasons for Creation	Hamilton modeled it after Bank of England Paid dividends and interest to government, which was the source of revenue	1811–1816 country in economic chaos following War of 1812 Explosion in number of unstable state banks
Function	Provided flexible currency Created adequate credit for business Generated revenue for national government	Controlled state banks Provided flexible currency Controlled inflation Restrained land speculation
Supporters	Alexander Hamilton's supporters Members of the Federalist Party Mercantile, eastern groups Friends of strong central government	Madison signed recharter National Republicans/Whigs Henry Clay/Nicholas Biddle Mercantile, eastern groups
Opponents	Thomas Jefferson's supporters (Democratic) Republicans Backcountry farmers States' rights supporters	Old Jeffersonians Andrew Jackson—Democrats Western farmers Small banking interests Land speculators
Reasons for Demise	Republicans gain political power and, by 1811, control Washington Madison's government did not renew charter	Andrew Jackson's veto Became a cause célèbre for opponents of Jackson Appeared undemocratic/elitist in the egalitarian 1830s
Constitutional Issue	Federalists: Bank was "necessary and proper" under "elastic clause" in Constitution Republicans: Bank violated the Constitution—establishing Bank was not enumerated as a power of Congress in Article 1, Section 8 Great struggle of loose vs. strict interpretation of the Constitution	1819 *McCulloch v. Maryland* declared the Bank constitutional 1832 Jackson declared the Bank unconstitutional in his veto message Part of an ongoing debate between the loose/strict interpretations of Constitution and the strong/weak views of federal government

Source Activities

Directions: Using the excerpt below and your knowledge of American history, answer the following questions.

> "It is to be regretted, that the rich and powerful too often bend the acts of government to their selfish purposes. Distinctions in society will always exist under every just government. Equality of talents, or education, or of wealth can not be produced by human institutions. In the full enjoyment of the gifts of Heaven and the fruits of superior industry, economy, and virtue, every man is equally entitled to protection by law; but when the laws undertake to add to these natural and just advantages artificial distinctions…to make the rich richer and the potent more powerful, the humble members of society—the farmers, mechanics, and laborers—who have neither the time nor the means of securing like favors to themselves, have a right to complain of the injustice of their Government."

—Andrew Jackson's veto message of National Bank Bill, July 1832

Multiple-Choice

1. Which of the following continuities from 1865–1900 most directly reflects the sentiment expressed in the passage?

    (A) farmers' attempts to institute currency reform

    (B) industrialists' attempts to raise protective tariff duties

    (C) Southern Redeemers attempts to expand states' rights

    (D) Eastern European immigrants' attempts to gain citizenship status

2. The ideas expressed in the passage above most closely resemble an earlier political debate over the

    (A) passage of the Sedition Act of 1798

    (B) approval of Alexander Hamilton's financial plan

    (C) ratification of the Jay Treaty

    (D) passage of the Tariff of 1816

Short-Answer

Using the excerpt, answer parts a, b, and c.

a) Briefly explain how ONE of the following actions was both a validation and a repudiation of President Jackson's economic program and philosophy:
- the veto of the National Bank
- the passage of the Specie Circular
- the creation of "pet" banks

b) Briefly explain how Jackson's Bank veto challenged past government economic policy from 1815–1829.

c) The National Bank was a source of political division in both the years 1791–1811 and 1816–1836. Briefly explain ONE important similarity in the opposition to its creation in both eras.

Lesson 8

Liberal and Conservative in United States History, 1790–1940

Two of the most misunderstood political terms in any U.S. history course are *liberal* and *conservative*. In general, liberals examine and challenge the existing attitudes and behaviors of their society and seek to change them. Conservatives, on the other hand, embrace the conventional wisdom of their times, accept the status quo, and support only small, incremental changes. These fundamental beliefs shaped the specific policies that liberals and conservatives endorsed during each era of U.S. history.

However, the two terms have a perplexing way of confusing students. Part of the difficulty is that their meanings have flip-flopped throughout the decades. For example, the liberal idea of early nineteenth-century Jeffersonians that government's involvement in society should be limited became a conservative belief during the twentieth century. And Alexander Hamilton's conservative idea of expanding the government's role in society during the 1790s to promote public interest was warmly endorsed by the liberals of the 1930s.

The chart on the next page will help you understand the shifting nature of liberal and conservative labels from 1790 to 1940. (The next section will examine the idea from 1940 to 1985). As you study the chart, try to formulate clearer definitions of *liberal* and *conservative*. Also, consider why the meaning of the terms changed so often during the course of U. S. history.

Directions: Analyze the chart on *liberal* and *conservative*, and then answer the following questions.

1. From 1790 to 1840 a liberal would have supported
   (A) the National Bank
   (B) limiting the power of governments
   (C) secession
   (D) a strong central government

2. A similarity between the conservatives of the 1790s and the liberals in the twentieth century was that both favored
   (A) government use of the spoils system
   (B) expanding the money supply by coining silver
   (C) an agrarian (farming) way of life
   (D) an active government involved in society

3. Which pair of issues divided liberals and conservatives from 1865 to 1900?
   (A) civil rights and the tariff issue
   (B) expansion of slavery and the National Bank
   (C) business regulation and road/canal construction
   (D) the money supply and business regulation

Dates	Liberal	Conservative
1790–1824	Thomas Jefferson spokesman Favored farmers Best government is the least government Advocated states' rights Opposed National Bank Supported low taxes/tariffs Supported reduced army and navy *Laissez-faire*	Alexander Hamilton spokesman Favored commercial, mercantile groups Government should be strong Wanted centralized government power Favored National Bank Believed that tariffs were necessary Strong national defense
1824–1840	Personal liberty, weak government Free competition, egalitarian opportunity Anti-National Bank, anti-tariffs States should fund roads, canals Supported Andrew Jackson	Supported compact theory of government Weak presidents Pro-National Bank National government should fund roads, canals Whigs—opponents of Andrew Jackson Supported Henry Clay
1840–1865	Pro-union Antislavery Favored national program of roads/canals Opposed westward expansion Opposed extending slavery into territories Opposed secession	States' rights Proslavery Opposed national program of roads/canals Favored westward expansion Favored extending slavery into territories Supported secession
1865–1900	Supported Radical Reconstruction Wanted honesty in government Supported Reform Darwinism Anti-imperialist Expanded money supply (paper, silver) Supported government regulation of business Wanted low tariffs	Resisted Radical Reconstruction Tolerated spoils system Supported Social Darwinism Expansionist Supported gold standard *Laissez-faire* High tariffs Gospel of Wealth
1900–1940	Government intervention in society Progressive social and labor reforms Regulations and limitations of trusts Collective security (League of Nations) Promoted consumer protection Presidents: T. Roosevelt, W. Wilson, and FDR Direct government relief/welfare in 1930s Square Deal, New Deal Low tariffs	Old Guard Republicans Extremely favorable to business interests Isolationism Leaders: Taft, Lodge, Harding, Coolidge, Hoover Rugged Individualism Normalcy in 1920s Best government is least government No direct relief or welfare High tariffs

Source Activities

Directions: Using the excerpt below and your knowledge of American history, answer the following questions.

> "There is a widespread belief among the American people that the great corporations known as trusts are harmful to the general welfare… It [the danger of corporations] is based upon the sincere belief that combination and concentration should be, not forbidden, but supervised and within reasonable limits controlled. In my judgment this belief is right.
>
> It is no limitation upon property rights or freedom of contract to require that when people receive from the government the privilege of doing business under corporate form, they should be truthful as to the value of the property in which capital is to be invested. Great corporations exist only because they are created and safeguarded by our institutions. It is therefore our right and our duty to see that they work in harmony with these institutions…In the interest of the public, the government should have the right to inspect and examine the workings of the great corporations engaged in interstate business…"

—Theodore Roosevelt on Trusts and Business Reform, 1901

Multiple-Choice

1. Which one of the following would most likely support the perspective expressed in the passage?
    - (A) a member of the Social Gospel movement
    - (B) a disciple of Herbert Spencer
    - (C) an advocate of *laissez-faire* Capitalism
    - (D) an opponent of Socialism in the United States

2. In their efforts to address the challenges noted above by President Roosevelt, progressive reformers
    - (A) nationalized many businesses and corporations
    - (B) asked corporations to downside voluntarily
    - (C) curtailed consolidation of corporations
    - (D) supported corporations in labor disputes

Short-Answer

Using the excerpt, answer parts a, b, and c.

a) Historians have discovered the roots of the Progressive Movement in the political developments after the Civil War. Briefly explain which ONE of the groups listed below contributed most to progressive thought from 1901–1917.

- Populist Party
- Greenback Labor Party
- Women's Christian Temperance Union

b) Contrast your choice against ONE of the other options, demonstrating why that option is not as good as your choice.

c) Both the years 1901–1917 and 1933–1941 saw an increase in government intervention in the economy. Briefly explain ONE important reason for a more active government response to economic problems in both time periods.

Lesson 9

Liberal and *Conservative* in United States History, 1940–1985

The division between liberals and conservatives continued after 1940. Liberals maintained their desire to promote change and to challenge the conventional thinking and behavior of their times. Conservatives adhered to their beliefs in protecting current societal norms and resisting sweeping, dramatic changes.

The post-World War II world presented the United States with a host of new challenges. The New Deal, while not ending the Depression, had transformed thinking about governmental domestic policy. The wartime alliance of England, the Soviet Union, and the United States collapsed quickly into a new East-West ideological rivalry. Liberals and conservatives divided over the best ways for the nation to address these foreign and domestic changes. Both groups grappled with the role of the United States in confronting the rising communist threat, the role of the government in regulating the economic life in the nation, and the pace of advancement for women and blacks in society. These issues would shape the postwar liberal-conservative debate.

The chart on the following page outlines the differences between liberal and conservative beliefs from 1940 to 1985. As you study it, look for consistent patterns of beliefs that each group held throughout the post-World War II years. Was one philosophy more consistent than the other? Also, was there a belief that conservatives embraced in one time period that became the liberal position in another? And vice versa?

Directions: Analyze the chart on *liberal* and *conservative*, and then answer the following questions.

1. From 1940 to 1985, conservatives consistently believed that
   (A) civil rights are a national priority
   (B) the role of the government in society should be limited
   (C) the New Deal should become a permanent part of American society
   (D) the Soviet Union is a trustworthy and dependable ally

2. A liberal in the 1960s would have supported
   (A) a declaration of war against North Vietnam
   (B) Mississippi's right to handle its own racial problems
   (C) a federal law protecting park lands
   (D) the use of federal troops to curb civil rights protest marches

3. A conservative during the 1980s would have supported a law that
   (A) raised income taxes by 20 percent
   (B) reduced the defense budget by 20 percent
   (C) increased research on alternative sources of energy
   (D) reduced taxes for married people

36 – *Threads of History*

Dates	Liberal	Conservative
1940–1960	Government should regulate economy Government responsible for people's welfare Deficit spending acceptable U.S. accepts international role Communism a challenge at home and abroad Supported organized labor Embraced federal support of racial justice and equality Encouraged flexible military response	Government should be limited in society Promoted individual responsibility for welfare Wanted a balanced budget Communism was a great domestic threat Limited overseas involvement but contained Communism with force Reconsidered much of the New Deal States should handle their racial issues Encouraged massive retaliation
1960–1968	Expanded role of government in society Wanted Vietnam to be a limited war Racial justice was national priority Protected the environment Women's rights important U.S. should end domestic poverty Youth culture tolerated and celebrated	Government should be limited in society Total military victory in Vietnam States handle racial problems Wanted to restore law and order in cities Upheld sexual/gender roles Defended traditional family values Youth culture deplored
1968–1975	Withdraw from Vietnam Promoted Equal Rights Amendment for women Richard Nixon and Watergate a threat to liberty Great Society must be maintained Blacks' gains must expand with busing and affirmative action Nixon should be impeached	Wanted limited government in society Peace with honor in Vietnam Maintained traditional gender roles 'Silent Majority' should be heard Watergate not that important Repealed much of Great Society No special treatment for minorities to achieve equality Maintained that Nixon was no more corrupt than earlier presidents
1975–1985	Maintain Great Society Insisted on human rights in foreign policy Avoid future Vietnams Détente with USSR Promoted affirmative action Supported Equal Rights Amendment Supported conservation of energy Supported abortion rights (*Roe v. Wade*)	Wanted limited government in society Cut taxes Increased defense spending Acted aggressively overseas USSR viewed as an "evil empire" Limited federal role in civil rights Maintained family values Stressed finding new sources of oil Prolife (anti-abortion)

Source Activities

Directions: Using the excerpt below and your knowledge of American history, answer the following questions.

> "During four futile years, the Administration...has talked and talked and talked the words of freedom, but it has failed and failed and failed in the works of freedom...failures mark the slow death of freedom in Laos; failure infest the jungles of Vietnam, and failure haunt the houses of our once great alliances...
>
> Rather than useful jobs in our country, our people have been offered bureaucratic "make work"; rather than moral leadership, they have been given bread and circuses. ...today in our beloved country we have an Administration which seems eager to deal with the Communism in every coin known—from gold to wheat, from consulates to confidences, and even human freedom itself.
>
> ...And I want to make this abundantly clear—I don't intend to let peace or freedom be torn from our grasp because of lack of strength or lack of will..."
>
> —Barry Goldwater at Republican Convention, 1964

Multiple-Choice

1. The ideas expressed in the passage most directly contributed to which of the following trends from 1980–1992?

    (A) the call for expanded civil rights for African Americans

    (B) a drive to balance the federal budget

    (C) a military buildup and challenge to the Soviet Union

    (D) the flow of political power from the President to Congress

2. Which of the following movements in the first half of the twentieth century would most directly support the argument made in the excerpt?

    (A) the movement to restrict the formation of trusts

    (B) the movement to limit the hours of women in factories

    (C) the movement to make the world safe for democracy

    (D) the movement to reduce government regulation and taxation

Short-Answer

Using the excerpt, answer parts a and b.

a) Historians have proposed that Barry Goldwater was influential in the conservative revival in the United States from 1975–1992. Briefly explain how TWO of the ideas expressed in the passage were translated into public policy in the last quarter of the twentieth century.

b) Briefly explain how ONE development from 1960–1964 that is *not* mentioned in the excerpt supported the author's argument.

Lesson 10

Political Parties in the Nineteenth Century

The founding fathers dreaded the formation of political parties in America. They feared that factions would corrupt and compromise the integrity of the government. Men such as James Madison and George Washington believed that political parties would undermine the foundation of a successful republic—the virtue of the people.

Nevertheless, parties formed quickly. Disagreements over Hamilton's financial plan, the nature of the Constitution, and the French-English conflict of the 1790s gave rise to the Federalist and Republican Parties. Thus, despite the fears of some leaders, by 1800 the United States had developed a full-fledged political party system.

The charts on the following two pages trace the evolution of the political parties during the nineteenth century and present their principles. Because the parties divided themselves into conservative and liberal positions, these materials should be used in conjunction with the chart on liberal and conservative beliefs from 1790 to 1940. As you study these materials, think about the political issues that have consistently divided Americans over the years, and consider whether parties serve any useful function in our political system.

Directions: Analyze the charts on political parties, and then answer the following questions.

1. A farmer who opposed the creation of the National Bank in the 1790s would likely join the
   (A) Democratic Republican Party
   (B) Democratic Party
   (C) Free Soil Party
   (D) Whig Party

2. The Federalist Party, the Whig Party, and the Republican Party of the 1850s all supported
   (A) government assistance to end slavery
   (B) government assistance to business interests
   (C) strict construction of the Constitution
   (D) an expansionistic foreign policy

3. A businessman in the 1840s who sought government assistance in building a road through his state would support the policies of the
   (A) Democratic Republican Party
   (B) Federalist Party
   (C) Populist Party
   (D) Whig Party

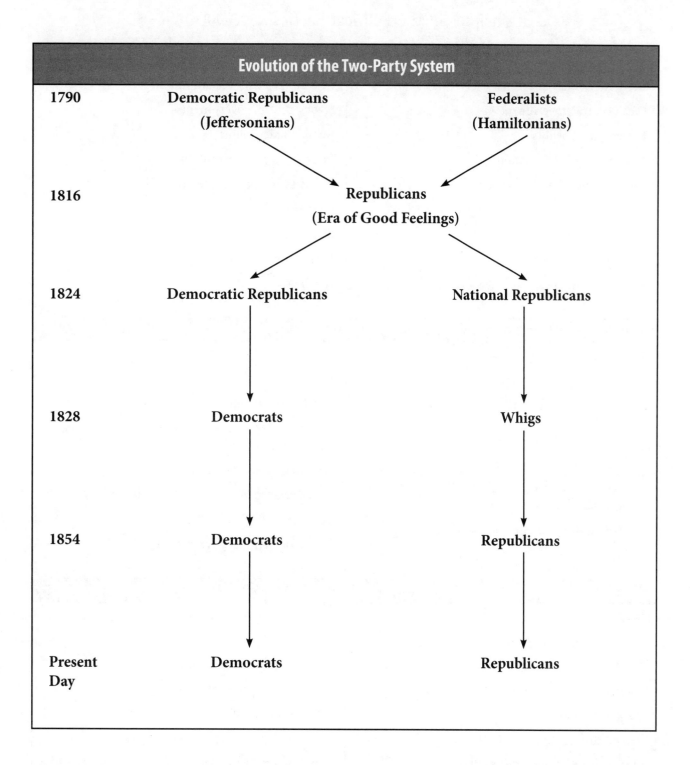

Lesson 10: Political Parties in the 19th Century - 41

Principles of the Political Parties, 1790–1900

Democratic Republicans (1790–1810)	Federalists (1790–1810)
Leader: Thomas Jefferson	Leader: Alexander Hamilton
Weak central government	Strong central government
Protect states' rights	Reduce states' rights
Strict view of Constitution	Loose view of Constitution
Agrarian oriented (pro-farmer)	Business and commerce oriented
Low taxes	High taxes
Weak military	Strong military
Anti-National Bank	Pro-National Bank
Pro-French	Pro-British

Jacksonian Democrats (1828–1848)	Whigs (1832–1852)
Jeffersonian traditions/ideas	Hamiltonian traditions/ideas
Supporters: small farmers and mechanics	Mercantile/business interests
Anti-National Bank	Pro-National Bank
States control/building of roads and canals	National government control/building of roads and canals (American System)
Proslavery	Opposed spread of slavery
Pro-Mexican War	Anti-Mexican War
Strong executive	Weak executive
Laissez-faire	Energetic national government

Democrats (1850–1900)	Republicans (1854–1900)
Proslavery	Opposed the spread of slavery
Favored secession from Union	Opposed secession
Blamed for Civil War (Bloody Shirt Issue)	Whig influence/pro-business
States' rights (especially on civil rights)	Briefly championed civil rights
Agrarian oriented	Business oriented
Feared strong central government	Supported active national government
Opposed gold standard (usually)	Supported gold standard
Used Spoils System	Used Spoils System but made some reforms
Supported lowering tariffs (1887)	Supported high tariffs
Reduced government role in railroad building	Government support in building railroads
In 1890s opposed Imperialism	In 1890s favored Imperialism

Source Activities

Directions: Using the excerpt below and your knowledge of American history, answer the following questions.

> "...The great object of the institution of civil government is the improvement of the condition of those who are parties to the social compact. ...For the fulfillment of those duties governments are invested with power, and to the attainment of the end—the progressive improvement of the conditions of the governed. ...I would suggest the expediency of connecting the equipment of a public ship for the exploration of the whole northwest coast of this continent. ...Connected with the establishment of a university, or separate from it, might be undertaken the erection of an astronomical observatory...
>
> But...if these powers and others enumerated in the Constitution may be effectually brought into action by laws promoting the improvement of agriculture, commerce, and manufactures, the cultivation and encouragement of the mechanic and of the elegant arts, the advancement of literature, and the progress of the sciences, ...to refrain from exercising them for the benefit of the people themselves...would be treachery to the most sacred of trusts..."
>
> —John Quincy Adams, Message to Congress, December 6, 1825

Multiple-Choice

1. For a supporter of the excerpt above, what change in America's political identity in the 1820s would be necessary to improve "the social compact?"
   - (A) broadening suffrage by eliminating property requirements in order to vote
   - (B) reducing the reach of the federal government in economic matters
   - (C) limiting the power of the judicial branch of government
   - (D) accepting an expansion of the elastic clause of the Constitution

2. The ideas expressed in the excerpt were later reflected in the political platform of the
   - (A) Democratic Party
   - (B) Anti-Mason Party
   - (C) Whig Party
   - (D) Liberty Party

Lesson 10: Political Parties in the 19th Century

Short-Answer

Using the excerpt, answer parts a and b.

a) Briefly explain how TWO of the following events gave rise to the political beliefs expressed in the excerpt:
- The conclusion of the War of 1812
- The promulgation of the Henry Clay's American System
- The re-charter of the Bank of the United States

b) Briefly explain ONE political development from 1824–1840 that challenged the point of view expressed in the excerpt.

Third Parties in United States History

Lesson 11

Third parties have played a peripheral, but important, role in the American political process. Although no third party has ever come close to winning the White House, some have played the role of spoiler. For example, in 1844, the Liberty Party won enough votes in New York State to cost Henry Clay the presidency. And in 1912, the Progressive Party (Bull Moose Party) split the Republican vote and assured Woodrow Wilson's election.

A more common role for third parties has been as a vehicle for groups to vent their anger and opposition to the political status quo. In many cases, third parties have introduced ideas that eventually gained acceptance by the two major parties. And once they delivered their message, these third parties faded away. Specifically, the Free Soil Party's opposition to the spread of slavery in the 1840s influenced the Republican Party's platform in the 1850s, and the Populist Party platform of the 1890s was a preview of the progressive Republican and Democratic Parties' agendas of the early nineteenth century. Similarly, both Democrats and Republicans embraced the American Independent Party's law-and-order message in the late 1960s and early 1970s. In many ways, the historian Richard Hofstadter was right when he suggested that third parties are like bees: once they sting, they die.

The charts on the following two pages look at the most influential third parties of the nineteenth and twentieth centuries. As you review them, think about ways the American political system has limited the role of third parties, yet has also created conditions that promote their formation.

Directions: Analyze the charts on third parties in United States history, and then answer the following questions.

1. The third party that provided the greatest influence on the progressive reformers of the early twentieth century was the
   - (A) American Independent Party
   - (B) Liberty/Free Soil Party
   - (C) Populist Party
   - (D) States' Rights Party (Dixiecrats)

2. Which of the following pairs of third parties represented an attempt to prevent changes in the racial policies of their times?
   - (A) the States' Rights Party (Dixiecrats) and the Populist Party
   - (B) the Liberty/Free Soil Party and the Populist Party
   - (C) the Progressive Party (Bull Moose) and the States' Rights Party (Dixiecrats)
   - (D) the American Independent Party and the States' Rights Party (Dixiecrats)

3. A factory worker in the 1840s who hoped to become a farmer in the nonslave territories of the West would likely support the ideas of the
   - (A) Populist Party
   - (B) Progressive Party (Bull Moose)
   - (C) States' Rights Party (Dixiecrats)
   - (D) Liberty/Free Soil Party

Third Parties in United States History

	Liberal Party, 1840–1848; Free Soil Party, 1848–1852	American Party (Know-Nothings), 1849–1856	People's Party (Populist), 1892–1903
Background	Grew out of split in abolitionist movement in late 1830s Liberty party merged into the Free Soil party in 1848	Grew out of nativist sentiment of the 1830s and 1840s Started as the "Supreme Order of Star-Spangled Banner"	Grew from farmer grievances against railroads and banks after the Civil War
Candidates	James Birney John P. Hale Martin Van Buren	Millard Fillmore	James B. Weaver William J. Bryan Tom Watson
Principles	Opposed the spread of slavery into territories Motto: "Free soil, free speech, free labor and free men" Free homesteads Repeal of Fugitive Slave Law End slavery in Washington, D.C.	Secrecy surrounded policies and members Immigration restrictions Anti-Catholic Literacy test to vote Tried to avoid a position on slavery (failed) Opposed Kansas-Nebraska Act	Free coinage of silver Public ownership of railroads/communications systems Income tax Eight-hour work day Immigration restrictions Direct election of U.S. senators
Impact	First political parties to oppose spread of slavery into territories Forerunners of the Republican Party of 1850s May have cost Henry Clay the 1844 election when Birney ran strong in New York State	Focused anti-immigrant, anti-Catholic resentment that had been building for years Briefly poised to replace Whigs as second national party Strong in Pennsylvania, New York, Massachusetts Eventually split over slavery	Omaha Platform of 1891 became blueprint for progressive reforms of twentieth century 1892 won 22 electoral votes Silver issue had little appeal to nonfarmers Failed to gain support of urban laborers

Third Parties in United States History

	Progressive Party (Bull Moose, 1912), 1912–1924	States' Rights Party (Dixiecrats), 1948	American Independent Party, 1968–1972
Background	Grew from split between William Taft and Theodore Roosevelt in 1912	Grew from Democratic platform plank in 1948 that endorsed a modest civil rights program	Grew from civil rights revolution in 1960s Reaction to urban, racial unrest and rioting in mid-1960s
Candidates	Theodore Roosevelt Robert M. LaFollette	Strom Thurmond	George Wallace
Principles	Antitrust action Regulation of business Conservation of natural resources Women's suffrage Lower tariffs Direct democracy—recall, initiative, referendum	States should control civil rights Retain segregation of the races Maintain Jim Crow system in South Strict interpretation of Constitution	Law and order States should control civil rights Maintain racial segregation Reduce government power in Washington Repeal much of the Great Society's War on Poverty All-out victory in Vietnam
Impact	Split Republican vote in 1912 elected Woodrow Wilson president Roosevelt rejoined the Republican Party; Progressive Party faded after election of 1924	Expected to cost Truman and Democrats the election but Truman won Carried four southern states with 39 electoral votes Beginning of decline of Democratic Party in South	Won 46 electoral votes Made both Republicans and Democrats toughen their law-and-order stands Gave voice to a "white backlash" against integration Anti-Washington message adopted by other conservatives

Lesson 11: Third Parties in U.S. History

Source Activities

Directions: Using the illustration below and your knowledge of American history, answer the following questions.

"The Grange Awakening the Sleepers," 1873

Multiple-Choice

1. The sentiment expressed in the cartoon most directly contributed to which of the following activities?
   - (A) farmers' attempts to de-regulate the railroads
   - (B) farmers' attempts to move to eastern cities
   - (C) farmers' attempts to break national railroad strikes
   - (D) farmers' attempts to challenge the economic status quo

2. The ideas expressed in the cartoon most directly reflect which of the following continuities in United States history?
   - (A) an attempt to reduce the declining status of farmers in America
   - (B) an attempt to increase the use of civil disobedience protest in America
   - (C) an attempt to reduce the power of trusts in America
   - (D) an attempt to increase the price of farm products in America

Short-Answer

Using the illustration, answer parts a, b, and c.

a) Explain the point of view reflected in the cartoon regarding ONE of the following:
   - An American farmer
   - A railroad executive
   - A passenger on the train

b) Explain how the point of view you explained in <u>part a</u> might conflict with ONE of the other two groups.

c) Cite and explain ONE political development in the last quarter of the nineteenth century that supported the action depicted in the cartoon.

Lesson 12

Freedom of the Seas and Wars with Europe

The United States has always defended its right to sail the seas. In exercising this right, however, America has periodically encountered difficulty, especially when its claims to maritime freedom intruded into general wars on the European continent. In 1793 and 1796, President George Washington proclaimed that, during European conflicts, the United States would avoid political and military alliances but would continue sailing the seas and maintaining commercial relations with all nations (see also Lesson 15, "Cornerstones of United States Foreign Policy").

This policy, while prudent and in the national interest, led to war on two occasions. In 1812 and 1917, events forced the United States to abandon its neutrality (so-called "isolationism") and to use force to defend its rights to freedom of the seas.

The chart on the following page outlines the background and events that led to America's entry into war in 1812 and 1917. As you review it and the chart on "Cornerstones of U.S. Foreign Policy" in Lesson 15, assess the wisdom of America's decision to remain neutral while asserting its right to sail into the European war zone. What factors did our leaders consider when they formulated and followed this policy? How did they define our national interests in 1812 and 1917?

Directions: Analyze the chart on wars with Europe, and then answer the following questions.

1. The United States' neutrality (isolationism) during the two European wars meant that America would
   (A) maintain commercial ties with Europe, but would not join military alliances
   (B) assist France, because such help was in America's national interest
   (C) join the side most likely to win the war
   (D) cease all connections with Europe until the war was over

2. The principal impact of the War of 1812 within the United States was the
   (A) quick uniting of the nation around the policies of President Madison
   (B) repudiation of the War Hawks in Congress
   (C) triumph of the Federalist Party in the election of 1812
   (D) division of the country along regional lines

3. In declaring war in 1917, the United States hoped to
   (A) eliminate Germany as a commercial rival
   (B) promote democracy in Europe
   (C) make a permanent alliance with France and England
   (D) eliminate Mexico as a threat to America's security

Wars with Europe

	War of 1812	The Great War (WWI) 1917
Background	France and England went to war in 1793 over European rivalries Both countries asked U.S. for assistance Both countries prohibited U.S. trade with the other U.S. refused and both countries seized American ships and cargoes England seized American men as well (impressment)	War began in Europe in July 1914 Central powers (Germany et al.) fought against Allied powers (France, England et al.) Both Germany and England blockaded their enemies German submarines sank shipping vessels without warning *[Jutlon was a Battle]* England searched American ships
President(s)	Thomas Jefferson James Madison	Woodrow Wilson
Action to Stay Neutral	Withheld trade by: • Embargo Act, 1807 • Nonintercourse Act, 1809 • Macon's Bill Number 2, 1810	Neutrality proclamation *Lusitania* protest *Sussex* pledge to stop the use of submarines against neutral shipping
Major Events	*Chesapeake-Leopard* clash in 1807 Thousands of men seized by British (1803–1812) Hundreds of American ships searched and seized by British and French	*Lusitania* sunk May 1915 (1,400 killed) *Sussex* pledge issued in 1916 Zimmerman note, 1917 (Germany proposed an alliance with Mexico against U.S.)
Outcome	War declared against England in June 1812	War declared against Germany in April 1917
Comments	War supported by South and West "War Hawks" like Henry Clay, John C. Calhoun, and Felix Grundy pushed the president into war, had hopes U.S. would gain Canada by victory New England shippers opposed war, calling it "Mr. Madison's War" War divided the country, yet Madison won re-election in 1812	Germany's unrestricted submarine warfare led to war with Germany England seized many ships but did not take lives U.S. waged war "to make world safe for democracy" U.S. did not formally join military alliance with England and France

Source Activities

Directions: Using the excerpt below and your knowledge of American history, answer the following questions.

> "The true question in controversy…involves the interest of the whole nation. It is the right of exporting the production of our own soil and industry to foreign markets. Sir, our vessels are now captured…and condemned by the British Courts of Admiralty, without event the pretext of having on board contraband of war…
>
> …For my part I am not prepared to say that this country shall submit to have her commerce interdicted or regulated by any foreign nation. Sir, I prefer war to submission.
>
> Over and above these unjust pretensions of the British Government, for many years past they have been in the practice of impressing our seamen, for merchant vessels; this unjust and lawless invasion of personal liberty, calls loudly for the interposition of this Government."
>
> —Felix Grundy, December 9, 1811

Multiple-Choice

1. The controversy highlighted in the passage developed, in part, because of the ideas expressed in

    (A) Thomas Jefferson's Declaration of Independence
    (B) George Washington's farewell address
    (C) James Madison's war message
    (D) John C. Calhoun's *Exposition and Protest*

2. The sentiment expressed in the passage would most likely be opposed by a

    (A) Southern slave-holder
    (B) Mid-Atlantic banker
    (C) New England shipper
    (D) Western farmer

Short-Answer

Using the excerpt, answer parts a and b.

a) Briefly explain how TWO of the following measures attempted to avoid both war and submission to Great Britain from 1807–1810:
- The Embargo Act (1807)
- The Non-Intercourse Act (1809)
- The Macon's Bill Number 2 (1810)

b) In the years 1803–1812 and 1914–1917, the United States faced challenges to its rights on the sea. Briefly explain ONE important similarity in the United States' response to challenges in both eras.

Lesson 13

Compromises and the Union

Compromise was an essential element in the creation and maintenance of American democracy during the nation's first century of existence. On four different occasions, the political process reached a critical impasse, and only through compromise was a serious crisis avoided. The issues of congressional representation, the extension of slavery, and the settlement of Reconstruction all threatened the nation's domestic tranquility and the Union itself. In each instance, however, a compromise was reached that defused the crisis and restored some measure of domestic harmony.

The chart on the next page offers an overview of the four major compromises in U.S. history through the era of Reconstruction. As you review the chart, consider whether the compromises and the temporary solutions they provided were really in the national interest at the time or whether it would have been better for the country to confront the issues directly at that moment. Also consider whether a democratic republic is more dependent on compromises than other forms of government.

Directions: Analyze the chart on compromises in American history, and then answer the following questions.

1. The Great Compromise of 1787 resulted in
   (A) a legislative branch just like the one created by the Articles of Confederation
   (B) agreement on representation and taxes that counted slaves as 3/5 of a person
   (C) a national government with a two-house legislative branch
   (D) a government that gave disproportionate power to the small states

2. A common element in the Compromises of 1820 and 1850 was that both
   (A) dealt with land areas acquired by war
   (B) were followed by three decades of domestic peace
   (C) combined earlier proposals to end the domestic slave trade
   (D) dealt with the extension of slavery into the territories

3. The Compromise of 1877 marked the end of
   (A) northern military occupation of the South
   (B) deep resentments over the Civil War
   (C) Republican presidential dominance
   (D) sectional discord over race issues

Four Major Compromises in U.S. History

	Great Compromise 1787	Missouri Compromise 1820	Compromise of 1850	Compromise of 1877
Issue	Representation in Congress	Admission of Missouri would disrupt Senate balance between free and slave states Should slavery extend into new territories?	Admission of California to Union Disposition of the territory acquired from Mexican War	Who won the presidency in the election of 1876?
Background	Congress was expected to be dominating branch of government Virginia Plan called for representation by population New Jersey Plan proposed equal representation	Missouri wanted to become the 12th slave state (11 free) Should slavery extend north of Ohio River line? What would happen regarding slavery in rest of Louisiana Territory?	Should slavery extend into the Mexican Cession? Should D.C. outlaw slavery and/or slave trade? Should the Fugitive Slave Law be strengthened? Should California be admitted as a free state? What should be done about Texas's disputed boundaries?	Three states sent two sets of election returns Democrat Samuel Tilden needed only one electoral vote to win *Close election* Commission gave all 20 disputed votes to Republican Rutherford Hayes South threatened new rebellion
Resolution	Two houses of Congress House based on population Senate has two senators from each state Combined the Virginia and New Jersey Plans	Missouri became slave state Maine became free state No slavery north of 36 degrees/ 30 minutes in Louisiana Territory	① California became free state ② Utah/New Mexico Territory organized by popular sovereignty ③ Stronger Fugitive Slave Law ④ Slave trade ended in D.C. ⑤ Texas's land claims denied, but U.S. will pay Texas' debt	Hayes given presidency Removal of troops from South Aid for Southern railroads Two Southerners in Cabinet Patronage jobs given to Southerners
Significance	Allowed Constitution to be written and approved	Postponed debate over spread of slavery for 30 years	Postponed the Civil War for ten years	Ended Radical/ Congressional Reconstruction

Lesson 13: Compromises and the Union - 55

Source Activities

Directions: Using the excerpt below and your knowledge of American history, answer the following questions.

> "I return to the question with which I began: How can the Union be saved? There is only one way. That is by a full and final settlement based on the principle of justice, of all the disputes between the two sections. The South asks for justice, simple justice. Less it ought not to accept. It has no compromise to offer but the Constitution, and no concession or surrender to make. It has already surrendered so much that it has little left to surrender.
>
> Such a settlement would remove all the causes of dissatisfaction. It would satisfy the South that it could remain honorably and safely in the Union. It would bring back the harmony and good feelings between the sections that existed before the Missouri question. Nothing else can finally and forever settle the questions at issue, end agitation, and save the Union."
>
> —John C. Calhoun, March 4, 1850

Multiple-Choice

1. The ideas expressed in the excerpt reflect a continuing controversy over
   - (A) the place of slavery in the Constitution
   - (B) the ability of the South to recover fugitive slaves
   - (C) the abolitionist movement's right to free speech
   - (D) the extension of slavery into the territories

2. A proponent of the ideas expressed in the passage would likely believe that
   - (A) the Constitution must be strictly interpreted
   - (B) the Constitution is an evolving document
   - (C) the Constitution is perpetual and could not be dissolved
   - (D) the Constitution supports the regulation of slavery

Short-Answer

Using the excerpt, answer parts a, b, and c.

a) Briefly explain how ONE of the following compromises was most effective in preventing a break-up of the Union:
- The 3/5 Compromise
- The Missouri Compromise
- The Compromise of 1833

b) Contrast your choice from <u>part a</u> against ONE of the remaining options by demonstrating why your choice is the best.

c) Briefly explain one other instance in United States history when a compromise (other than the three mentioned in <u>part a</u>) was necessary to achieve a political settlement.

Lesson 13: Compromises and the Union - 57

Lesson 14

Judicial Nationalism, 1819–1824

The Federalists' political influence declined after the election of 1796. The party lost the White House in 1800 when Thomas Jefferson defeated John Adams. The War of 1812 further eroded Federalist political strength until, by 1818, Federalists represented less than one third of the Senate and House. Finally, by the election of 1820, there was no Federalist candidate to challenge James Monroe for the presidency. Thus, during the Era of Good Feelings (a.k.a. the National Period), the Federalists ceased to be a political force.

However, the Federalists' political ideology reached beyond 1820. The judiciary branch became a Federalist stronghold from 1801 to 1835, largely because of John Marshall. Appointed to the Supreme Court in 1801 by John Adams, Marshall served as Chief Justice until 1835. Throughout this time, he championed the twin Federalist goals of strengthening the central government and promoting business interests.

The Federalist philosophy was alive and well on the Supreme Court during the Era of Good Feelings (1816–1824). Three decisions in particular demonstrated how the Court strengthened the national government and encouraged business development. The chart on the following page summarizes these three important cases. As you study the chart, think about how Marshall, the lone Federalist on the Supreme Court for most of his tenure, could exert such influence in this era of Republican Party dominance. Further, how did the Supreme Court reflect the election returns from 1816–1824?

Directions: Analyze the chart on judicial nationalism, and then answer the following questions.

1. A significant impact of the Marshall Court decisions was to
   (A) expand the power of state governments at the expense of the national government
   (B) establish a confederation system of government where the states controlled the national political agenda
   (C) expand the powers of the national government at the expense of state governments' powers
   (D) promote economic conditions that benefited agrarian interests at the expense of mercantile interests

2. From 1819 to 1824, the Marshall Court favored business development with rulings that
   (A) put regulations into the hands of business-friendly state governments
   (B) restrained the restrictive regulations of the federal government
   (C) lowered property and corporate taxes
   (D) strengthened the partnership between financial interests and the federal government

3. The Marshall Court supported American nationalism from 1819 to 1824 by
   (A) eliminating the property requirement for voting
   (B) strengthening the central government's ability to direct and standardize economic policy
   (C) making American business competitive with other nations around the world
   (D) providing financial support for the "American System" of internal improvements

Threads of History

Influential Cases for Judicial Nationalism

	Dartmouth College v. Woodward, 1819	*McCulloch v. Maryland,* 1819	*Gibbons v. Ogden,* 1824
Background	New Hampshire Republicans wanted to rid Dartmouth College of its Federalist influence Changed charter and fired president of college	Maryland wanted to regulate a branch of National Bank within its borders Placed a tax on all banks in state not chartered by the legislature Bank refused to pay tax	New York granted a monopoly on ferry boat service between New York and New Jersey to Robert Fulton's steamboat company Others challenged the monopoly New York courts upheld the monopoly
Question(s) to be decided	Could a state change a private college into a public university by revoking its charter?	Could Maryland tax a branch of National Bank? Was Bank constitutional?	Was monopoly legal? What powers to regulate interstate commerce did federal government have?
Ruling	New Hampshire could not revoke Dartmouth's charter because it was a form of contract	Maryland could not tax bank because state power was subordinate to Constitution Court said "power to tax involves the power to destroy" Bank constitutional under necessary-and-proper clause	A federal coastal license nullified New York's grant of monopoly Congress had power to regulate interstate commerce Commerce was more than exchange of goods; it included transportation and other types of commercial endeavors
Business Interest Promoted	Contract law strengthened by extending contract clause to corporate charter Sanctity of contracts encourages commercial growth	Upheld National Bank, which was very popular among mercantile groups National Bank encourages commerce, business growth	Struck down monopolies, encouraging business competition Strengthened federal government's power over interstate commerce (more business friendly than states)
States' Rights Diminished	New Hampshire could not change college from private to public	Maryland's taxing power reduced	New York's power to regulate trade reduced

Source Activities

Directions: Using the excerpt below and your knowledge of American history, answer the following questions.

> "...[the] mass of evidence stands opposed to those constructions which are laboring to invest the federal government with powers to abridge the state right of taxation; to control states by a power to legislate for ten miles square; to expend money belonging to the United States without control; to enrich a local capitalist interest at the expense of the people; to create corporations for abridging state rights; to make roads and canals; and finally to empower a complete negative over state laws and judgments, and an affirmative power as to federal laws."
>
> —John Taylor's *New Views of the Constitution of the United States*, 1823

Multiple-Choice

1. In their efforts to address the challenges noted in the excerpt, the Jacksonians of the 1830s
   - (A) supported the Supreme Court's use of judicial review
   - (B) restricted states in developing internal improvements
   - (C) restricted the government's role in the economy
   - (D) supported the removal of Native Americans westward

2. Which of the following twentieth-century issues most closely parallels the controversy described in the passage?
   - (A) the question of protecting African-American civil rights
   - (B) the question of protecting the national environment
   - (C) the question of ownership of natural resources off of the Continental Shelf
   - (D) the question of where to store nuclear waste from power plants

Short-Answer

Using the excerpt, answer parts a, b, and c.

a) Briefly explain the main points made in the passage.

b) Briefly explain how ONE of the decisions of John Marshall's court in the 1820s reinforced many of the concerns about the role of the federal government expressed in the passage.

c) The Supreme Court often issued controversial rulings concerning the role of the federal government in American society. Briefly explain ONE decision that caused controversy and debate from 1856–1896.

Lesson 15

Cornerstones of United States Foreign Policy

Throughout its existence, the United States has established consistent principles of behavior toward various parts of the world. This consistency has been shaped by geography, domestic politics, and the unique features of each overseas region. During its first 150 years, America built three distinct foreign policies in Europe, Asia, and South America.

The chart on the following page provides an overview of the cornerstones of U. S. foreign policy: isolationism in Europe, the Monroe Doctrine in South America, and the Open Door in Asia. Each of these policies changed in some ways during the second half of the twentieth century as America emerged from World War II as a superpower with a dedication to containing Soviet Communism. This chart should be used in conjunction with the charts on containment of Communism in Lesson 33, America's role in Vietnam in Lesson 34, and the chart of famous doctrines in Lesson 35. Together, these charts review both the continuity and change in America's basic foreign-policy principles.

As you study this chart, consider several questions. How did the United States define its national interest in each of the three areas of the world? What specific regional and cultural conditions shaped America's foreign-policy response in each area? Are there consistent threads of interest that run through all aspects of U.S. foreign policy?

Directions: Analyze the chart on cornerstones of American foreign policy, and then answer the following questions.

1. One consequence of the Monroe Doctrine was that

    (A) Russia decided to ally with the United States to keep other European nations out of South America

    (B) England and America clashed repeatedly over their foreign interests during the nineteenth century

    (C) the doctrine forced America into unwanted European alliances

    (D) America became increasingly aggressive in enforcing the doctrine in the Western Hemisphere

2. The United States believed its Open Door Policy was threatened when countries tried to

    (A) achieve exclusive trading rights in various regions of China

    (B) spread foreign ideologies among the Chinese people

    (C) establish multilateral trade arrangements in China

    (D) spread Christianity among the Chinese people

3. A common characteristic of the three American foreign policy cornerstones was that all of them

    (A) promoted friendships with European powers

    (B) resulted in large territorial acquisitions for the United States

    (C) were issued to protect American interests

    (D) were directed toward American interests in Asia

Cornerstones of U.S. Foreign Policy

	Isolationism	Monroe Doctrine	Open Door
Area of World	Europe	Western Hemisphere	Asia
Year Established	1793, 1796	1823	1899–1900
Author(s)	George Washington	James Monroe John Quincy Adams	John Hay
Background	Proposed when England and France went to war 1793 Both countries expected our help U.S. had an alliance with France from Revolution	U.S. feared Spanish recolonization in South America U.S. feared Russian colonies on west coast of U.S. England wanted to be a partner in issuance; U.S. said no to dual authorship	After Spanish War (1898) U.S. became interested in China Europeans were already in China and had created trading spheres of influence that could exclude U.S.
Elements	Neutrality in European affairs No entangling military or political alliances for U.S. Europe/U.S. have separate spheres of interest Commercial relations maintained	No new colonies in Western Hemisphere. Existing colonies left alone by U.S. Isolationism from Europe reinforced from earlier foreign policy pronouncements Discouraged extension of monarchies into Americas	All nations share equal trading rights in China All countries must guarantee China's territorial integrity
Comments	Washington's Farewell Address in 1796 reinforced ideas Resulted in war in 1812, 1917 Established a policy that lasted until 1949 when U.S. joined NATO Cited as reason to oppose League of Nations in 1919	England enforced doctrine for 70 years Roosevelt Corollary (1904) strengthened it U.S. became policeman of Caribbean "Big Stick" to keep down "chronic wrongdoing" Later became "Dollar Diplomacy" to control of the Caribbean region U.S. aggressiveness alienated many South American countries	U.S. became protector of China, but mainly sought trade access Boxer Rebellion (1900) frightened U.S. because China's territory might be divided by European powers Japan became greatest threat to Open Door When U.S. challenged Japan's violation of Open Door, Japan attacked Pearl Harbor

Source Activities

Directions: Using the cartoon below and your knowledge of American history, answer the following questions.

Puck Magazine, 1906

Multiple-Choice

1. The attitude expressed in the cartoon was most directly caused by the
   - (A) closing of the frontier in the late nineteenth century
   - (B) imperialist spirit in the late nineteenth century
   - (C) economic turmoil in the late nineteenth century
   - (D) debate over free silver in the late nineteenth century

2. The sentiment expressed in the cartoon most directly contributed to which of the following?
   - (A) United States activism in the South American/Caribbean regions
   - (B) United States acceptance of international cooperation in the South American/Caribbean region
   - (C) United States involvement in European affairs rather than the South American/Caribbean region
   - (D) United States withdrawal of aid to the South American/Caribbean region

Short-Answer

Using the cartoon, answer parts a, b, and c.

a) Explain how ONE of the following individuals or groups in the early twentieth century would respond to the sentiment expressed in the cartoon:
   - An American President from 1898–1920
   - A European Head of State from 1898–1920
   - The Native populations of South and Central America from 1898–1920

b) Briefly explain how ONE of the remaining individuals or groups not selected would counter the sentiment you selected in <u>part a</u>.

c) Briefly explain how ONE development in the years 1930–1965 challenged the point of view expressed in the cartoon.

Lesson 16

Expansion of the United States, 1783–1853

One of the dominant forces of American history during the first half of the nineteenth century was the nation's relentless march westward. Nearly every president from George Washington to Franklin Pierce promoted and encouraged geographic expansion. The United States sought to expand its borders through purchase and treaties, but when countries would not relinquish territory peacefully, armed force was often deployed.

Although these acquisitions were intended to strengthen and unite the nation, the new territories eventually disrupted the political process and divided the nation. By the 1840s and 1850s, "Manifest Destiny," with its call for an empire from the Atlantic to the Pacific Oceans, became intertwined with the expansion of slavery, and this issue tore the country apart and brought on the Civil War.

As you examine the chart and map of U.S. expansion on the next two pages, think about the factors that propelled American expansion. Try to list them in order of importance and defend the hierarchy you have established. Also, consider why the United States, a country that believed in self-determination, imposed its will on areas where other governments and cultures were already established?

Directions: Analyze the chart and the map on American expansion, and then answer the following questions.

1. Which pair of acquisitions completed America's Manifest Destiny?
   (A) Louisiana Purchase and Florida Purchase
   (B) Mexican Cession and Oregon Treaty
   (C) Treaty of Paris and Oregon Treaty
   (D) Florida Purchase Treaty and Mexican Cession

2. A common characteristic of the Treaty of 1783 and the Louisiana Purchase Treaty was that both
   (A) resulted in land losses for Great Britain
   (B) cost the United States no money
   (C) led to war with France
   (D) helped secure control of the Mississippi River

3. In terms of cost per square mile, which of the following acquisitions was America's poorest land deal?
   (A) Louisiana Purchase Treaty
   (B) Florida Purchase Treaty
   (C) Gadsden Purchase Treaty
   (D) Oregon Treaty

Threads of History

U.S. Expansion

Land Area	Date	Means of Acquisition	Cost	Significance
Original thirteen states and area east of Mississippi River	1783	Treaty of Paris with England to conclude the American Revolution	$0	U.S. gained trans-Appalachian empire Gateway to land beyond Mississippi River Led to Northwest Ordinance
Louisiana Territory	1803	Treaty with Napoleon in France	$15 million	Doubled the size of the U.S. Gave United States control of Mississippi River (New Orleans) Eliminated Napoleon as threat to American security Led to conflicts over status of slavery in new territories
Florida	1819	Adams-Onís Treaty with Spain (Transcontinental Treaty)	$5 million	Set Sabine River as southern boundary of U.S. Established boundary between New Spain and Louisiana Territory Spain recognized U.S. claims to Oregon U.S. surrendered its claims to Texas
Oregon	1846	Treaty with England	$0	Prevented war with England by splitting Oregon Territory at 49th parallel Gave U.S. clear claim to land on the Pacific Coast U.S. now stretched from ocean to ocean
Mexican Cession	1848	Treaty of Guadalupe Hidalgo settled Mexican-American War	$15 million	U.S. acquired California and large portions of southwest North America Completed Manifest Destiny Led to conflict over status of slavery in territory won from Mexico
Gadsden Purchase	1853	Treaty with Mexican government	$10 million	Bought with the hope of building a transcontinental railroad across the southern U.S. Instead, transcontinental railroad went through middle of the nation in 1860s

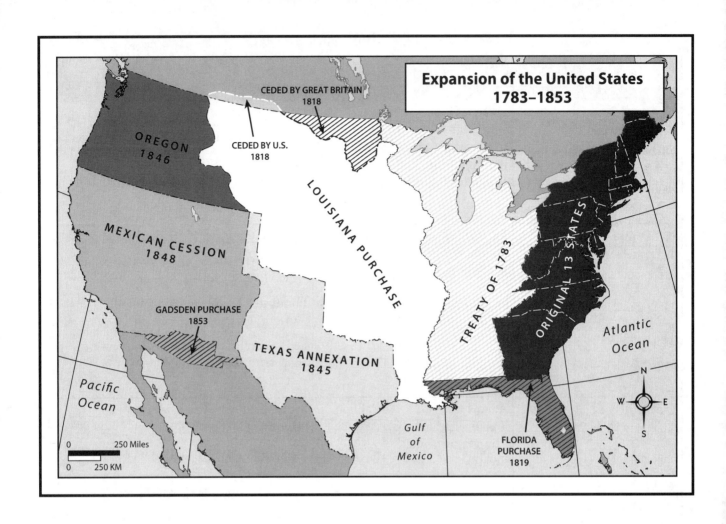

Source Activities

Directions: Using the excerpt below and your knowledge of American history, answer the following questions.

> "It is time now for opposition to the annexation of Texas to end. It is time for the common duty of patriotism to the country to take over. …The sweep of our eagle's wing already includes its fair and fertile land.
>
> If we needed a reason for taking Texas into the Union, it surely is to be found in the manner in which other nations have interfered in the matter. Their object is to oppose our policy and hold back our power, to limit our greatness, and to check the fulfillment of our manifest destiny to spread over the continent…
>
> The independence of Texas was complete and absolute. And these people will have a right to independence—to self government, to possession of homes conquered from the wilderness by their own labors and dangers, sufferings, and sacrifices…"
>
> —John L. O'Sullivan, "Annexation," Democratic Review, July–August 1845

Multiple-Choice

1. The ideas expressed in the passage reflect earlier debate over how to
   (A) preserve United States neutrality in European wars
   (B) avoid the waning of patriotism during the War of 1812
   (C) protect the Western Hemisphere from foreign countries
   (D) justify the acquisition of Louisiana and Florida

2. The ideas expressed in the excerpt most closely show the influence of which of the following beliefs?
   (A) that America had purchased the territory in question
   (B) that America had a Constitutional right to expand
   (C) that America was better suited than Europe to rule others
   (D) that America had a divine right to expand

Short-Answer

Using the excerpt, answer parts a, b, and c.

a) Briefly summarize the main points of the passage.

b) Briefly explain how ONE of the following resulted from the Mexican-American War and how it helped divide the nation in the 1850s:
- The Wilmot Proviso
- The Compromise of 1850
- The rise of "Slave Power"

c) Briefly explain how the sentiments expressed in the passage are similar to the point of view adopted by the United States in world affairs from 1890–1910.

Lesson 17

Wars in United States History

Although the United States has professed its dedication to peace, much of its history has been shaped by armed conflicts with other countries. Most of the nineteenth-century clashes resulted from America's attempt to establish and enhance its place in the world. On the other hand, as it matured in the twentieth century, the United States fought principally to maintain its position in the world community and to defend its many overseas interests.

The charts on the following two pages present the eight wars in which the United States was involved in the 163 years between 1812 and 1975. The chart should be studied in conjunction with the materials on "Freedom of the Seas" in Lesson 12, "Expansion of the United States" in Lesson 16, and "Major Treaties in United States History" in Lesson 22. As you study the two charts of warfare, compare the conflicts of the nineteenth century with those of the twentieth century. What similarities do you see in them? What differences do you notice? How did America's opponents change in the two centuries? How did the causes of the conflicts change? Would you have difficulty defending the proposition that Americans are a peaceful people?

Directions: Analyze the charts on the wars in American history, and then answer the following questions.

1. Both the Mexican War and Spanish-American War resulted in
    (A) little territory lost or gained by the belligerents
    (B) completion of America's drive for Manifest Destiny
    (C) stopping European aggression in the Caribbean and South America
    (D) the United States gaining significant territorial acquisitions

2. In terms of objective and outcome, the war that most resembled the Korean War was
    (A) Vietnam
    (B) World War II
    (C) the Spanish-American War
    (D) World War I

3. The War of 1812, the Spanish-American War, and World War I all involved
    (A) disputes over land claims in the Western Hemisphere
    (B) toppling foreign leaders who threatened United States security
    (C) maritime incidents that led to war
    (D) border incidents that started the conflicts

	War of 1812	Mexican War	Civil War	Spanish-American War
Dates	1812–1814	1846–1848	1861–1865	1898
President(s)	James Madison	James K. Polk	Abraham Lincoln	William McKinley
Causes	Impressment Freedom of the seas threatened U.S. hoped to gain Canada from England War Hawks' pressure	Manifest Destiny Texas boundary dispute South's desire for new slave territory	Slavery States' rights Eleven southern states withdrew from Union to start their own country	Oppression of Cubans by Spain sparks revolt U.S. business interests threatened in Cuba by the fighting between the rebels and Spanish Battleship Maine blown up Yellow press strengthened anti-Spanish sentiment Pressures of new Manifest Destiny
Important Military Events	England burned Washington Plattsburg battle Battle of the Thames Siege of Baltimore New Orleans	Buena Vista Siege of Veracruz Mexico City	Antietam Fredericksburg Chancellorsville Gettysburg Vicksburg Sherman's march to sea	Manila Bay San Juan Hill
Treaty	Ghent	Guadalupe Hidalgo	Appomattox	Paris
Terms	No resolution of original disputes No territory gained for either side	U.S. got Mexican Cession Agreement on Texas border	South rejoined the Union, but without slavery	Cuba freed from Spain U.S. got Guam, Puerto Rico, Philippines
Importance	War promoted American nationalism and patriotism Crushed Indian resistance in South and West Federalist Party died Industrialization began in New England Era of Good Feelings began	Fulfilled Manifest Destiny Re-opened debate over expansion of slavery (Wilmot Proviso) Led to Compromise of 1850	Union saved Ended slavery in the U. S. Bloodiest war in American history Difficult and divisive Era of Reconstruction left bitter feelings on both sides for decades	U.S. acquires foreign territory and becomes world power U.S. enforced Monroe Doctrine with aggressiveness

	World War I	World War II	Korean War	Vietnam
Dates	1917–1918	1941–1945	1950–1953	1950–1975
President(s)	Woodrow Wilson	Franklin D. Roosevelt Harry Truman	Harry Truman Dwight Eisenhower	Harry Truman to Gerald Ford
Causes	German submarine attacks Sinking of the *Lusitania* Zimmerman Note Trade, cultural ties with Britain Make "world safe for democracy"	Japan closed Open Door in China Japanese expansion in Asia and Pacific Pearl Harbor attacked Germany declared war on U.S.	Communist North Korea attacked South Korea and the United States sent troops to contain communism	Failure to hold Geneva Accords' elections in 1956 caused communist insurgency in South Vietnam and attacks by North Vietnamese forces
Important Military Events	Belleau Wood Chateau Thierry Second Battle of the Marne Meuse-Argonne	Guadalcanal Midway Leyte Gulf El Alamein Stalingrad Normandy Invasion Battle of the Bulge	Pusan siege Inchon landing Chinese communist intervention	Gulf of Tonkin Pleiku Tet Attacks Invasion of Cambodia
Treaty	Versailles	Accords with the Axis powers	Panmunjom Accords	Paris Accords
Terms	Germany surrendered, punished for war League of Nations created European boundaries redrawn to create new nations	Unconditional surrender Germany, Italy and Japan gave up Fascist philosophies and methods Japan and Germany occupied by Allied forces	South Korea remained free of Communism Communism remained in the North	Cease fire Communist troops remained in South Americans withdrew South Vietnam temporarily remained free of Communism
Importance	Four empires destroyed Communists took over in Russia U.S. rejected membership in League of Nations Harsh treatment of Germany leads to rise of Hitler	Atomic age began at Hiroshima USSR/U.S. began Cold War United Nations founded U.S. became international superpower	First test of military containment First limited war Hardened relations between the U.S. and Communist China	Six U.S. presidents tried to contain Communism War divided nation, left legacy of distrust of government and foreign intervention In 1975 North conquered South and Communism triumphed

Lesson 17: Wars in United States History

Source Activities

Directions: Using the excerpt below and your knowledge of American history, answer the following questions.

> "...In my generation, this was not the first occasion when the strong had attacked the weak. I recalled some early instances: [Japan in] Manchuria, [Italy in] Ethiopia, [Germany in] Austria. I remembered how each time that the democracies failed to act it had encouraged the aggressors to keep going ahead.
>
> Communism was acting in Korea just as Hitler, Mussolini, and the Japanese had acted ten, fifteen, and twenty years earlier. I felt certain that if South Korea was allowed to fall, Communist leaders would be emboldened to override nations closer to our shores. If the Communists were permitted to force their way into the Republic of Korea without opposition from the free world, no small nation would have the courage to resist threats and aggression. ...If this was allowed to go unchallenged it would mean a third world war, just as similar incidents had brought on the second world war..."
>
> —Memoirs of Harry S. Truman: 1946–52, Years of Trial and Hope, 1956

Multiple-Choice

1. Which of the following individuals would be most likely to support the perspective of the excerpt?
   - (A) an opponent of foreign aid
   - (B) a proponent of massive retaliation
   - (C) an opponent of the United Nations
   - (D) a proponent of collective security

2. The sentiment expressed in the passage led the United States in the 1950s and 1960s to
   - (A) acquire overseas areas that provided vital natural resources
   - (B) withdraw military assistance from non-democratic countries
   - (C) send military aid and forces overseas
   - (D) exploit political unrest within the Soviet block countries

Short-Answer

Using the excerpt, answer parts a, b, and c.

a) Briefly explain how ONE of the following actions was most effective in implementing George Kennan's ideas of containment:
- The Truman Doctrine
- The Marshall Plan
- The North Atlantic Treaty Organization

b) Briefly explain ONE development in the period 1945–1950 that is not included in the passage, and explain how it supported President Truman's point of view.

c) Briefly explain ONE criticism of United States policy toward the Soviet Union from 1945–1950.

Lesson 18

Amendments to the Constitution

The amendments to the Constitution are an important but sometimes overlooked aspect of the United States history survey course. Usually students examine the first ten amendments in conjunction with the struggle over the ratification of the Constitution between 1787 and 1788. The opponents of the Constitution (anti-Federalists) complained that the document lacked a Bill of Rights and demanded this omission be corrected in order for ratification to proceed. Amendments also figured prominently in events during Reconstruction (1865–1877) and the early 1920s.

The chart on the next page is a quick summary of the twenty-seven amendments to the Constitution. As you study them, consider several questions. First, how did the first ten amendments reflect America's anxieties about government that developed during the colonial and revolutionary periods? Secondly, why were the Thirteenth, Fourteenth, and Fifteenth Amendments the most revolutionary of all the changes to the Constitution? Finally, how did the Eighteenth and Nineteenth Amendments represent both an extension and a termination of progressive reforms?

Directions: Analyze the chart on amendments to the Constitution, and then answer the following questions.

1. The first ten amendments to the Constitution were intended to
   (A) protect rights that were perceived as threatened during the colonial period
   (B) reestablish a republican form of government in the United States
   (C) strengthen the national government's ability to protect law and order
   (D) restore the national government's control over the economy

2. As a result of the Fifteenth, Nineteenth, and Twenty-sixth Amendments, the United States government
   (A) limited suffrage to white, native-born citizens
   (B) strengthened its commitment to the ideals of the Declaration of Independence
   (C) tried to increase suffrage for literate citizens
   (D) drew closer to the original intent of the Constitution regarding suffrage

3. During the 1950s and 1960s, which of the following amendments provided the basis for court action to expand and protect civil rights for African-Americans?
   (A) Thirteenth Amendment
   (B) Twenty-fourth Amendment
   (C) Eighteenth Amendment
   (D) Fourteenth Amendment

76 - *Threads of History*

	Amendments to the Constitution
1	Prohibits federal government from restricting religion, speech, assembly, petition, press
2	Gives citizens right to bear arms
3	Prohibits federal government from housing troops in private homes during peacetime
4	Prohibits federal government from making unreasonable searches and seizures
5	Prohibits double jeopardy, self-incrimination, seizing property without due process, and just compensation
6	Citizens have right to speedy and public trial, be informed of charges against them, impartial jury, legal counsel
7	Citizens have right to a jury trial
8	Prohibits excessive bail or fines and cruel or unusual punishment
9	Rights not enumerated in Constitution remain in people's hands
10	Powers not delegated to federal government are reserved to the state or people
11	Federal courts have no authority in suits by citizens against another state or foreign states
12	Provides for separate electoral voting for president and vice president
13	Abolished slavery in the United States
14	Blacks given citizenship; all citizens guaranteed due process of law and equal protection of the law; federal government would protect rights if states failed to do so
15	Black men given the right to vote
16	Federal government allowed to tax incomes
17	Direct popular election of United States senators
18	Prohibited the manufacture, sale, and transportation of alcoholic beverages
19	Women given the right to vote
20	Congress begins new term on January 3; president and vice president begin terms on January 20 of year following their election
21	Repealed Eighteenth Amendment
22	Limited the president to two terms or ten years in office
23	District of Columbia given three electoral votes in presidential elections
24	Abolished poll taxes in the voting process
25	When president dies or is disabled, vice president becomes president and new vice president is appointed; established procedures in case of presidential disability
26	All citizens eighteen years of age and older given right to vote
27	Congress prohibited from changing its pay for the current congressional term

Source Activities

Directions: Using the excerpt below and your knowledge of American history, answer the following questions.

> "All persons born or naturalized in the United States, and subject to the jurisdiction thereof, are citizens of the United States and the State wherein they reside. No State shall make or enforce any law which shall abridge the privileges or immunities of citizens of the United States; nor shall any State deprive any person of life, liberty, or property, without due process of law, nor deny any person within its jurisdiction the equal protection of the laws."
>
> —The Fourteenth Amendment, Section 1, 1868

Multiple-Choice

1. The principles expressed in the Fourteenth Amendment led most directly to which of the following continuities in the twentieth century?
   - (A) recognition of group identities and rights in society
   - (B) recognition of the superiority of one group over another
   - (C) recognition that only native born groups had equal legal protection
   - (D) recognition that group identities should be discounted in all cases

2. The ideas expressed in the Amendment most clearly reflect the influence of which of the following?
   - (A) earlier judicial decisions that restricted suffrage
   - (B) earlier judicial decisions that stated that only white people had legal rights
   - (C) earlier judicial decisions that restricted self incrimination
   - (D) earlier judicial decisions that stated that citizenship alone conferred suffrage

Short-Answer

Using the excerpt, answer parts a and b.

a) Select TWO amendments to the United States Constitution and explain how collectively they helped form and strengthen an American identity.

b) Briefly explain why the amendments selected are a better choice than ONE of the other options available in the Constitution.

Lesson 19

Utopian Societies in the 1830s and 1840s

In the 1830s and 1840s, a number of experimental communities arose in the United States. Historians have often labeled these societies "utopian" because of their goals and practices, and their hopes to create perfect social, political, and economic relationships among their members. Some groups drew their inspiration from the secular philosophies of Robert Owen and Charles Fourier or from the writings of the Transcendentalists. Other groups followed strict religious principles and beliefs. All, however, attempted to find an alternative to the competitive, socially flawed (as they viewed it) world of the 1830s and 1840s.

By the early 1840s, over eighty communal experiments existed in the United States. Fueled by the Panic of 1837, and a general spirit of reform, these societies tended to feature rural, communal living, egalitarian gender relations, and cooperative, rather than competitive, economic systems. Some also embraced innovative and occasionally shocking family and sexual practices. Only a few lasted into the 1850s and 1860s, as their ideals conflicted with the economic and social realities of day-to-day living.

The chart on the following two pages outlines five of the most prominent utopian societies. As you study it, think about the conditions in America in the 1830s and 1840s that gave rise to disillusionment with mainstream society. Also, consider why the groups failed to sustain their living experiments over a long period of time.

Directions: Analyze the chart on utopian societies, and then answer the following questions.

1. One common principle shared by all the societies in the 1830s and 1840s was their

   (A) support of complex marriages
   (B) rejection of capitalism and private property
   (C) support of the ideas of Charles Fourier
   (D) dedication to improving both the mind and body

2. If a person put diet and food at the center of his or her reform ideals, he or she would be most comfortable joining

   (A) New Harmony
   (B) Brook Farm
   (C) Oneida
   (D) Fruitland

3. The most common reason for the decline of these societies was their

   (A) inability to overcome internal conflicts and dissension
   (B) refusal to set up any type of economic planning
   (C) unpatriotic behavior as America expanded westward
   (D) unorthodox sexual ideas and practices

Five Prominent Utopian Societies

	Founders	Location/Background	Principles/Practices	Reasons for Decline
New Harmony 1825-1828	Robert Owen	Harmonie, Indiana Former site of George Rapp's Harmonie Society.	Hoped to create "new moral world" Organized "phalanxes" Employed industrial Socialism Advocated communal living/ child rearing Defended women's rights	Intense infighting Insolvency No clear lines of authority Area was prone to flooding.
Brook Farm 1841-1847	George Ripley Sophia Ripley	Concord, Massachusetts Attracted literary figures: Nathaniel Hawthorne, Margaret Fuller, Bronson Alcott Hawthorne wrote about it in *The Blithedale Romance* (1852)	Based on Transcendentalism Daily life consisted of manual labor combined with intellectual seminars Advocated "high thinking /plain living" In 1845 embraced Fourierism: created "phalanxes" (community property and living)	Intellectuals disliked farm work Fire destroyed Phalanstery (meeting house) in 1846 Series of illnesses ravaged community in 1845-1846
Fruitland 1843-1844	Bronson Alcott Charles Lane	Harvard, Massachusetts Lasted from June 1843–January 1844 Never more than 30 members	Followed transcendental principles—commune with nature Believed that diet is key to a good life: ate no animal substances, milk, honey, cheese, coffee, or tea Lived on fruit, bread, water Rejected Capitalism	Failed to establish agricultural self-sufficiency Alcott and Lane were poor leaders Coming winter ended the experiment

Five Prominent Utopian Societies

	Founders	Location/ Background	Principles/ Practices	Reasons for Decline
Shakers Communities 1830-1860 (peak years)	Mother Ann Lee *(later)* Joseph Meacham Lucy Wright	Originated in England. In the U.S., established in Lebanon, NY. By 1840s, settlements stretched from Maine to Kentucky. At peak had 6,000 members	God was both Father/Mother. Both men and women equal in the eyes of God. Celibacy was ideal; men and women lived apart, but could eat together. Rejected accumulation of private property. Ann Lee was the daughter of God. Women had leadership roles in communities. Marketed vegetables, flower seeds, and fine furniture	Reached peak membership in 1840. Did not grow internally through live births. Gained new members only through conversion, indenturing children, adoption
Oneida 1848-1880	John H. Noyes	Central New York State. Grew to about 300 members. An economic success produced silk products, steel traps, silverware	Banned private property. Communal property holdings. Practiced "mutual criticism" of members. Practiced a form of eugenics. Enacted "complex marriages"—multiple sexual partners	Noyes fled to Canada, charged with adultery. 1879: stopped practicing complex marriages. 1881: became a joint stock company

Lesson 19: Utopian Societies in the 1830s and 1840s

Source Activities

Directions: Using the excerpt below and your knowledge of American history, answer the following questions.

> In order more effectually to promote the great purposes of human culture; to establish the external relations of life on a basis of wisdom and purity; ... we the undersigned do unite in a voluntary Association...
>
> Article I
>
> Sec. 2. No member of the Association shall ever be subjected to any religious test; nor shall any authority be assumed over individual freedom of opinion by Association, nor by one member over another; ...
>
> Article III
>
> Sec. 1. The Association shall provide such employment for all its members as shall be adapted to their capacities, habits, and tastes; and each member shall select and perform operations of labor...as shall be deemed suited to his own endowments...
>
> Sec. 2. The Association guarantees to all its members, their children and family dependents, house-rent, fuel, food, and clothing, and the other necessaries of life, without charge, ...
>
> Article IV
>
> Sec. 2. The General Direction and Direction of Education shall be chosen annually, by the vote of the majority. ...The Direction of Finance shall be chosen annually, by the vote of the majority of the share-holders and members of the Assocation...
>
> —The Constitution of the Brook Farm Association, 1841

Multiple-Choice

1. Which of the following twentieth-century developments most closely paralleled the interpersonal relationships proposed in the excerpt?

(A) 1960s experiments in communal living
(B) 1930s government attempts to promote racial understanding
(C) 1920s efforts to promote self-help and personal advancement
(D) 1950s attempts to reduce gender differences

2. The ideas expressed in the passage most closely show the influence of which of the following?

(A) beliefs in America's destiny to expand
(B) beliefs in self-government and liberty
(C) beliefs in limitations on religious freedom
(D) beliefs in checks and balances to maintain liberty

Short-Answer

Using the excerpt, answer parts a, b, and c.

a) Briefly explain why ONE of the following sets of writings would have been out of place in the library at Brook Farm:
- Joseph Smith's *Book of Mormon*
- Adam Smith's *The Wealth of Nations*
- Benjamin Rush's *Thoughts Upon Female Education*

b) Briefly explain ONE element of life at Brook Farm that was different from mainstream society in the 1840s.

c) Briefly explain ONE economic development from 1815–1845 that may have promoted the formation of societies such as Brook Farm.

Lesson 19: Utopian Societies in the 1830s and 1840s

Expanding Democracy— The Abolitionist Movement

The period from 1830 to 1860 was a time of social and political reform in the United States. Reformers such as Dorothea Dix, Horace Mann, and Elizabeth Cady Stanton attempted to change the way the country treated the mentally ill, educated its children, and viewed women. All these efforts, however, were dwarfed by the attempt to end slavery. Prodded by the British antislavery movement and the Second Great Awakening, Americans began establishing abolitionist societies during the early 1830s. The American abolitionist movement was united for a brief period of time, but, by the early 1840s, fissures had appeared in its leadership and tactics.

The chart on the next page outlines the three distinct strands of the abolitionist crusade. As you look at the chart, consider how the abolitionists found common areas of agreement with one another, yet disagreed over the means to achieve their goal of ending slavery in America.

Directions: Analyze the chart on abolitionist movements in America, and then answer the following questions.

1. Many abolitionists challenged the goals of the American Colonization Society because the organization

    (A) had the support of most freed blacks and reduced their loyalty to other abolitionist groups

    (B) was deeply religious, while most abolitionists were nonbelievers

    (C) attempted to eliminate the free black population rather than end slavery itself

    (D) called for penal and temperance reform, which detracted from abolitionism

2. William Lloyd Garrison clashed with the American and Foreign Anti-Slavery Society because he

    (A) supported forming a political party to end slavery

    (B) was very religious and sought close ties to the churches to end slavery

    (C) was too timid in his methods to end slavery

    (D) supported full participation for women in the crusade against slavery

3. An abolitionist in the 1840s who sought to end slavery by political means and supported paying slaveholders for their lost property would join the

    (A) American Colonization Society

    (B) American and Foreign Antislavery Society

    (C) American Antislavery Society

    (D) American Bible and Temperance Society

84 - *Threads of History*

Strands of the Abolitionist Crusade

	American Colonization Society	American Antislavery Society	American/Foreign Antislavery Society
Year Started	1817	1833	1840
Leader(s)	Robert Finley Henry Clay James Madison	William Lloyd Garrison	Theodore Weld Lewis and Arthur Tappan
Goals	Voluntary emancipation and colonization Colonize free blacks in Africa Establish a colony in Africa for freed people	Immediate emancipation of all slaves in America No compensation to the slave holders	Gradual emancipation of all slaves in America Compensation to the owners for the loss of their slaves
Means	Lobbied Congress for support Gained $100,000 from Congress to establish Liberia Published appeals for freed people to colonize in Africa	Moral persuasion Paid agents to lecture on the evils of slavery Publication of an antislavery paper, *The Liberator* Opposed political action	Moral persuasion Paid agents and published a newspaper to rally support Worked with churches Political action—close to the Liberty Party
Women's Role	Not an issue	Full, equal participation Women should address both men and women at meetings	Limited role, mostly behind the scenes Feared male backlash if women were too prominent in meetings
Summary/ Comments	Established Liberia in 1823 Congress mandated that all captured slave ships return Africans to Liberia About 15,000 free black people colonized in Liberia 1817–1870 Most free blacks opposed organization and its efforts	Garrison's radicalism made him controversial and divisive Challenged the churches to attack slavery from pulpit Condemned Constitution because it condoned slavery Challenged the Union itself Involved in many reforms besides slavery	Moderate approach; viewed Garrison as too radical, split with him in 1840 Attracted older members Tried to use Liberty and Free Soil Parties to gain members Declined in late 1840s and disbanded in 1855

Source Activities

Directions: Using the excerpt below and your knowledge of American history, answer the following questions.

> "…The corner-stone upon which they founded the Temple of Freedom was broadly this— 'that all men are created equal; that they are endowed by their Creator with certain inalienable rights; that among these are life, LIBERTY, and the pursuit of happiness…'
>
> …those, for whose emancipation we are striving—constituting at the present time at least one-sixth of our countrymen, —are recognized by the laws, and treated by their fellow beings, as marketable commodities— as goods and chattels—as brute beasts; —are plundered daily of the fruits of their toil without redress; —really enjoy no constitutional nor legal protection from licentious and murderous outrages upon their persons; …
>
> We…maintain—That no man has a right to enslave or imbrute his brother—to hold or acknowledge him, for one moment, as a piece of merchandise…"
>
> —William Lloyd Garrison, "Declaration of Sentiments of the American Anti-Slavery Convention," December 1833

Multiple-Choice

1. What direct action did the abolitionists take to try to correct the wrongs outlined in the excerpt?
   - (A) They established newspapers and made speeches against slavery.
   - (B) They elected anti-slavery senators to Congress.
   - (C) They worked to change the membership of the Supreme Court.
   - (D) They worked to create Jim Crow laws to protect African-American rights.

2. The sentiment expressed in the passage clearly shows the influence of earlier religious beliefs that
   - (A) religion had little impact on changing society
   - (B) the Declaration of Independence and religion were connected
   - (C) personal and societal salvation were connected
   - (D) personal and societal salvation were pre-determined

Short-Answer

Using the excerpt, answer parts a, b, and c.

a) Select ONE of the individuals below and explain how he might oppose the ideas expressed by William Lloyd Garrison:
- John Calhoun
- David Walker
- Lewis Tappan

b) Defend your choice from <u>part a</u> by contrasting it with ONE of the two remaining individuals.

c) Americans sought to expand freedom and equality in the years 1830–1865 and 1950–1970. Briefly explain ONE important similarity in the reasons why this quest emerged in both of these time periods.

Lesson 20: Expanding Democracy—The Abolitionist Movement - 87

Lesson 21

Women's Movement during the Nineteenth Century

The nineteenth century witnessed many attempts to reform and improve America. One of the most controversial of these reforms was the women's movement. Women struggled to overcome their social, economic, and political positions of inferiority in American society. The women who led this crusade came mainly from the ranks of the abolitionists. In fact, before the Civil War, the three most significant women leaders—Elizabeth Cady Stanton, Susan B. Anthony, and Lucretia Mott—focused most of their efforts on the battle against slavery.

Women faced many hurdles in their quest for full citizenship. Legal barriers prevented women from voting or serving on juries, and economic laws and traditions, such as coverture, gave husbands complete control over their wives' economic lives. Moreover, women had to combat not only legal obstacles but psychological ones, because most women accepted their inferior place and status in American society. Women were expected to adhere to the values of the Cult of Domesticity and True Womanhood, values that equated true womanhood with submissiveness to men and devotion to family. Stanton, Mott, and others faced great difficulty in raising women's awareness of the injustice of a male-dominated society.

The chart on the following page outlines the three major strands of the women's movement during the nineteenth century. As you study it, identify the issues that united women and the ones that divided them. Also, consider why women targeted suffrage as their primary goal.

Directions: Analyze the chart on the nineteenth-century women's movement, and then answer the following questions.

1. The women's movements of the nineteenth century were united around the belief that

    (A) black men's voting rights were more important than women's suffrage

    (B) controlling the use of alcohol was the key to gaining full equality for women

    (C) men were reliable allies in women's crusade for equality

    (D) gaining the right to vote was critical to women's advancement in America

2. A major split developed in the women's movement after the Civil War over

    (A) the use of petition and convention to achieve women's goals of equality

    (B) women working outside the home in jobs traditionally done by men

    (C) the interpretation of the Fifteenth Amendment

    (D) creating a third party only for women

3. The "Cult of Domesticity and True Womanhood" referred to

    (A) women accepting existing societal expectations for themselves

    (B) women forming groups to make homes cheerful for returning soldiers

    (C) women promoting the image of strong individuals capable of maintaining their households without any hired help

    (D) women expanding their sphere of interest and activities outside the home

Threads of History

Major Strands of the Nineteenth Century Women's Movement

	Seneca Falls Movement	National Woman Suffrage Association	American Woman Suffrage Association
Leaders	Elizabeth Cady Stanton Lucretia Mott	Elizabeth Cady Stanton Susan B. Anthony	Lucy Stone Julia Ward Howe
Goals	Right to vote Lessening economic oppression for women Overcoming "Cult of Domesticity and True Womanhood"	Right to vote along with black men Women should be included in 15th Amendment Wide range of reforms	Keep nation aware of women's suffrage, but accept black men as voters for time being 16th Amendment for women's suffrage
Supporters	Middle class women Some male abolitionists such as Frederick Douglass Quakers	Young, educated women Many from Seneca Falls Women in western states Only allowed women officials	More conservative women Strong in Boston area Former abolitionists: Frederick Douglass Welcomed male members
Methods	Published a Declaration of Sentiments Held an annual convention until the beginning of the Civil War	Lobbied to be included in 15th Amendment Later demanded a separate amendment to give women the right to vote	State-by-state approach Worked exclusively for women's suffrage Avoided reforms not directly related to right to vote
Comments	Meetings grew from the snubbing of Mott and Stanton at the World Anti-Slavery Convention in London Women asked James Mott to preside because they felt it inappropriate for a woman to do so	Most radical of women's groups Issued racist rhetoric against the 15th Amendment Hurt by association with Victoria Woodhull Merged with AWSA in 1890, becoming the National American Woman Suffrage Association (NAWSA)—Anthony and Stanton took leadership roles	More accepting of status quo Closer to the ideals of the "Cult of True Womanhood" Merged with NWSA in 1890, becoming the National American Woman Suffrage Association (NAWSA)—Anthony and Stanton took leadership roles

Lesson 21: Women's Movement during the 19th Century

Source Activities

Directions: Using the cartoon below and your knowledge of American history, answer the following questions.

Puck Magazine, June 6, 1894

Multiple-Choice

1. The point of view expressed in the cartoon is that
   (A) women should be arrested when they try to vote
   (B) women could depend on men to help them gain the vote
   (C) women should take care of their children and stop worrying about the vote
   (D) women would face social and legal barriers in gaining the vote

2. Which of the following mid-nineteenth century reforms most closely resembles the cause presented in the cartoon?
   (A) the movement to establish utopian communities
   (B) the movement to complete America's Manifest Destiny
   (C) the movement to change divorce laws
   (D) the movement to establish equal schools for men and women

Short-Answer

Using the cartoon, answer parts a, b, and c.

a) Briefly explain how ONE of the following individuals would respond to the point of view expressed in the cartoon:
   - Susan B. Anthony
   - Frederick Douglass
   - Catherine Beecher

b) Briefly explain how ONE of the other individuals in <u>part a</u> that you did not select would respond to the individual that you did select.

c) Briefly explain ONE important social or political response in the twentieth century to the conditions depicted in the cartoon.

Lesson 21: Women's Movement during the 19th Century

Lesson 22

Major Treaties in United States History

As the United States expanded, completed its continental consolidation, and involved itself in world affairs, conflicts with other nations arose. These diplomatic and military disputes grew more numerous and serious as America grew in size, power, and influence, and became more active in international affairs. The nation sought to resolve these clashes and disagreements through treaties and international agreements. The chart on the next two pages summarizes the major diplomatic pacts negotiated and signed by the United States from 1794 to 1954.

You should study the chart in conjunction with Lesson 12, "Freedom of the Seas and Wars with Europe;" Lesson 15, "Cornerstones of United States Foreign Policy;" Lesson 16, "Expansion of the United States 1783–1853;" and Lesson 17, "Wars in United States History." Collectively these materials provide a picture of America's diplomatic and military relations with the rest of the world. As you review these materials, evaluate the proposition that, in the long run, America accomplished more at the negotiating table than on the battlefield.

Directions: Analyze the chart on major diplomatic pacts, and then answer the following questions.

1. A common outcome in the Adams-Onís Treaty, the Treaty of Guadalupe Hidalgo and the Treaty of Paris 1898 was that all three
   - (A) ended wars with major European powers
   - (B) were settled without cash payments by the United States
   - (C) resulted in territorial acquisition for the United States
   - (D) were rejected by the U.S. Senate

2. Both the North Atlantic Treaty Organization and the Southeast Asia Treaty Organization were designed to
   - (A) stop the spread of Communism
   - (B) involve the United Nations in preserving peace around the world
   - (C) acquire spheres of influence in Asia for the United States
   - (D) keep Communism out of South America

3. The Treaty of Versailles was a unique agreement in U.S. history because it was the only major treaty
   - (A) that resulted in the acquisition of land for the United States
   - (B) that respectfully recognized Germany's rights in central Europe
   - (C) that was promoted and accepted by both political parties
   - (D) that was rejected by the U.S. Senate

Diplomatic Pacts, 1794–1954

Treaty	Nations	Provisions
Jay Treaty, 1794	United States/ England	Britain withdrew from forts in Great Lakes Arbitration of Revolutionary debts Payment for American shipping losses U.S. gained improved trading status with Britain
Treaty of Ghent, 1814	United States/ England	Ended War of 1812 No land concessions by either side No apology by British for impressment Established commission to set boundary between U.S./Canada
Adams-Onís Treaty, 1819	United States/ Spain	U.S. got Florida U.S. paid Spain $5 million Spain recognized U.S. claims to Oregon country Established boundary between New Spain and Louisiana Territory U.S. surrendered its claims to Texas
Treaty of Guadalupe Hidalgo, 1848	United States/ Mexico	Ended Mexican War Mexico recognized Texas annexation Mexico surrendered Mexican Cession U.S. paid Mexico $15 million
Treaty of Paris, 1898	United States/ Spain	Ended Spanish-American War Cuba freed from Spanish rule U.S. got Puerto Rico and Guam from Spain U.S. paid $20 million for Philippines
Treaty of Versailles, 1919	Allies/ Germany	Ended the Great War (World War I) Established the League of Nations Germany punished for starting war U.S. Senate rejected the treaty because of League of Nations and isolationist sentiment in U.S.
North Atlantic Treaty Organization, 1949	United States/ Twelve European Countries	Military alliance to contain Communism in Europe An attack on one country treated as an attack on all A mutual defense pact organized around concept of collective security First entangling alliance for the U.S.
Southeast Asia Treaty Organization, 1954	United States Great Britain France Australia New Zealand Thailand Pakistan Philippines	Mutual defense pact intended to repel common dangers in southeast Asia Committed to protecting countries under pressure from internal subversion and external attack by Communists Helped South Vietnam, Laos, and Cambodia Intended to contain Communism in Asia

Source Activities

Directions: Using the cartoon below and your knowledge of American history, answer the following questions.

The Evening Star, Washington, D.C., September 5, 1919

Multiple-Choice

1. Which of the following individuals would most likely support the perspective of the cartoon?

    (A) a person who completely rejected membership in the League of Nations

    (B) a person who rejected the Treaty of Versailles, but accepted membership in the League

    (C) a person who accepted membership in the League, but with some changes to its structure

    (D) a person who accepted membership in the League without question or change

2. Which of the following consequences most directly resulted from the actions shown in the cartoon?

    (A) The United States supported the ideas of collective security.

    (B) The United States retreated into traditional isolationism toward Europe.

    (C) The United States strengthened its aid to downtrodden people in the world.

    (D) The United States proclaimed its policy of containment of Communism.

94 - *Threads of History*

Short-Answer

Using the cartoon, answer parts a, b, and c.

a) Briefly explain how ONE of the following individuals would react to the sentiments expressed in the cartoon:
- Henry Cabot Lodge
- William Borah
- Woodrow Wilson

b) Briefly explain how ONE of the other individuals you did not select in <u>part a</u> would challenge the position of your choice.

c) Briefly explain ONE development in the period 1933–1945 that challenged the point of view of the cartoon.

Lesson 22: Major Treaties in United States History

Lesson 23

Reconstruction of the South

When the Civil War ended in 1865, many questions arose about the political and physical rebuilding of the eleven southern states that had attempted to leave the Union in 1861. During the next three years, the country was convulsed in conflict about Reconstruction. The most contentious issue of the era was the future of the former slaves. The overriding theme of this struggle was whether President Andrew Johnson or the Radical Republicans would decide the fate of the defeated South and freed people.

The political battle became so heated that, in 1868, President Johnson was impeached. Although the radical Republicans in Congress could not convict him, they gained control of Reconstruction and attempted to revolutionize many of the social and political relationships in the United States.

The chart on the following page offers a concise summary of the major issues and elements of the competing Reconstruction plans. As you study the chart, think about how the plans would appeal to the following groups: freedmen, southern planters, northern Democrats, poor southern whites, moderate northern Republicans, abolitionists, western farmers, and northern factory workers.

Directions: Analyze the chart on reconstruction plans for the American South, and then answer the following questions.

1. The congressional Reconstruction plan proposed at the end of the Civil War found little support among
   (A) former abolitionists
   (B) teachers in the Freedmen's Bureau
   (C) former slaves
   (D) states rights' supporters

2. A major difference between presidential and congressional Reconstruction was that
   (A) the presidential plan did not punish the South at all and the congressional plan did
   (B) the congressional plan expanded the powers of the central government to protect the rights of the former slaves and the presidential plan did not
   (C) the presidential plan allowed the South to rejoin the Union with slavery unchanged and the congressional plan required emancipation
   (D) the presidential plan provided for a Freedmen's Bureau and the congressional plan did not propose a similar organization

3. A major shortcoming of the congressional plan for Reconstruction was that it failed to
   (A) grant black men the right to vote
   (B) put troops in the South after the war
   (C) end slavery
   (D) give land to the former slaves

Reconstruction Plans for the American South

	Presidential	Congressional
Who was in charge?	President Abraham Lincoln President Andrew Johnson	Thaddeus Stevens Charles Sumner Other radical Republicans
Dates	April–December 1865	1866–1877
Had the South left the Union?	No; executive branch believed it needed to restore the states to their proper relationship with the Union	Yes; the southern states had left the Union, were conquered territories, and should be treated accordingly
Acts/Actions	Proclamation of Amnesty and Reconstruction 1863, 1865 Vetoed Wade Davis Bill 1864 Pardoned most ex-Confederates Thirteenth Amendment 1865	Civil Rights Act 1866 Renewed, expanded Freedmen's Bureau Fourteenth Amendment 1868 Reconstruction Acts 1867–1868 Tenure of Office Act 1867 Fifteenth Amendment 1870 Force Acts 1870–1871 Civil Rights Act 1875
Elements of Plans	South must: • renounce secession • ratify Thirteenth Amendment • 10% of voters from 1860 must swear allegiance to Union • Confederate officers, officials, wealthy must make special request for pardon	South must: • ratify Thirteenth, Fourteenth, and Fifteenth Amendments • accept black citizenship • accept black men voting Confederate officials, officers, soldiers could not vote Put 20,000 troops in the South Civil Rights Act of 1875 provided for social integration
Aid for Freedmen	None provided; up to the individual states to decide how and to what extent newly freed slaves would be helped	Created Freedmen's Bureau, providing welfare and education to former slaves Provided troops to protect black voting rights No permanent land distribution, which gave rise to sharecropping and tenant farming

Source Activities

Directions: Using the excerpt below and your knowledge of American history, answer the following questions.

> "…A majority of Congress desires that treason shall be made hateful, not by bloody executions, but by other adequate punishments. …I am speaking of granting the vote to Negroes in the rebel states. Have not loyal blacks as good a right to choose rulers and make laws as rebel whites? In the second place, it is a necessity in order to protect the white people who are loyal to the Union in the seceded states…
>
> But it will be said, as it has been said, "This is Negro equality!" What is Negro equality about? It means, as understood by honest Republicans, just this much and no more: Every person, no matter what his or her race or color, every human being who has an immortal soul, has an equal right to justice, honesty and fair play. …The same law which condemns or acquits Africans should condemn or acquit white people…"
>
> —Thaddeus Stevens to the U.S. House of Representatives, January 3, 1867

Multiple-Choice

1. Which of the following actions would most directly support Stevens' argument in the excerpt above?
   - (A) the passage of the 14th and 15th Amendments
   - (B) the creation of the Freedmen's Bureau
   - (C) the change in property requirements in voting
   - (D) the abolition of slavery in the United States

2. The ideas expressed in the passage most clearly reflect the influence of which of the following?
   - (A) economic principles expressed in the Constitution
   - (B) natural rights principles expressed in the Declaration of Independence
   - (C) political principles expressed in the Articles of Confederation
   - (D) moral principles expressed in the many colonial constitutions

Short-Answer

Using the excerpt, answer parts a, b, and c.

a) Briefly explain how ONE of the following attempted to punish the South by modifying group identity from 1865–1877:
- The Freedmen's Bureau
- The Fourteenth Amendment
- The Fifteenth Amendment

b) Briefly explain ONE reason why some Americans objected to this modification and punishment.

c) Briefly explain ONE political or social response from 1877–1900 that attempted to negate the sentiment expressed in the passage.

Lesson 24

Judicial Betrayal—The Road to *Plessy v. Ferguson*

When the Supreme Court ruled in 1896 that "separate but equal" facilities for blacks and whites were constitutional in public transportation, the ruling was the culmination of the Court's role in gradually narrowing the interpretation of the Fourteenth Amendment. (See Lesson 18 for a summary of this amendment.) It also gave judicial approval to the Jim Crow system that separated the races in social and cultural settings during the decades following the Civil War. The trend of the Court's decisions from 1870 to 1900 was to restrict the scope of the Fourteenth Amendment, especially its "equal protection" clause for African Americans. By the time of *Plessy*, the nation was in full retreat from the Reconstruction era pledge of full equality for all citizens regardless of race.

The chart on the following page summarizes the four major cases that defined the Court's attitude toward civil rights after the Civil War. In *Plessy*, the majority ruled that "legislation is powerless to eradicate racial instincts or to abolish distinctions based upon physical differences." Can you describe the events from 1877 to 1896 that gave rise to this line of thinking?

Directions: Analyze the chart on the four major civil rights cases, and then answer the following questions.

1. From 1873 to 1896, the general trend of the Supreme Court decisions regarding civil rights was to
    - (A) support the idea that all men were created equal
    - (B) make no distinction between public and private discrimination
    - (C) uphold black rights in all cases of discrimination
    - (D) narrow the interpretation of the Fourteenth Amendment

2. Which of the following groups would likely agree with and support the Supreme Court decisions on civil rights from 1873 to 1896?
    - (A) Southern blacks
    - (B) radical Republicans
    - (C) loose constructionists of the Constitution
    - (D) strict constructionists of the Constitution

3. When the Supreme Court issued its "separate but equal" decision in *Plessy v. Ferguson*, it provided support for the
    - (A) spoils system
    - (B) Jim Crow system
    - (C) American System
    - (D) Lowell labor system

Major Civil Rights Cases

Case	Date	Background	Question to be Answered	Ruling
Slaughterhouse cases	1873	Louisiana created state-sanctioned monopolies in slaughterhouse business—butchers believed their 14th Amendment rights were being violated	Did 14th Amendment expand the federal government's authority to protect black citizens?	No, defense of most rights still a job for individual states 13th and 14th Amendments did not greatly expand power of U.S. government 14th Amendment did not create new set of national citizenship rights
U.S. v. Cruikshank	1876	Colfax Massacre resulted in 100 black deaths/ 3 whites killed—no one convicted	Did the 14th Amendment protect blacks from private acts of violence?	No, 14th Amendment did not give U.S. government power to suppress ordinary crimes by individuals U.S. involved only when state actions denied citizen rights
U.S. v. Singleton	1883	Black man denied entry into an opera house in New York City	Did Civil Rights Act of 1875 prohibit private acts of discrimination?	No, Civil Rights Act of 1875 was unconstitutional 14th Amendment only dealt with state discrimination; did not cover private acts of discrimination
Plessy v. Ferguson	1896	Black man tried to sit in "white" railcar to test Louisiana's Jim Crow laws	Did Jim Crow system violate 14th Amendment?	No, legislation was powerless to stop private acts of racial bias Separate facilities were not inherently unconstitutional Facilities could be separate if they were equal

Lesson 24: Judicial Betrayal—The Road to *Plessy v. Ferguson*

Source Activities

Directions: Using the excerpt below and your knowledge of American history, answer the following questions.

> "...The Court holds that the 14th Amendment applies only to state action. ... Individual invasion of individual rights is not the subject matter of the [14th] Amendment...
>
> The wrongful act of an individual, unsupported by any such [state] authority, is simply a private wrong, or a crime of that individual; an invasion of rights of the injured party, it is true...; but if not sanctioned in some way by the state, or not done under state authority, his rights remain in full force, and may presumably be vindicated by resort to the laws of the state for redress."
>
> —Civil Rights Cases, 1883

Multiple-Choice

1. Which of the following developments resulted most directly from the principles established by the ruling?
   - (A) the rise of racial self-help groups such as the National Urban League
   - (B) the rise of a strong Republican Party in the southern states
   - (C) the rise of racial violence in the southern states
   - (D) the rise of committees to reduce racial prejudice in southern states

2. The Court decision excerpted above was likely written in response to the claim that
   - (A) separate but equal schools were unconstitutional
   - (B) the federal government should expand its defense of citizen's rights
   - (C) every American should have the right to vote
   - (D) states were powerless to defend the rights of their citizens

Short-Answer

Using the excerpt, answer parts a, b, and c.

a) Briefly explain how ONE of the following individuals would react to the decision presented in the passage:
- J. Strom Thurmond
- Thurgood Marshall
- W.E.B. DuBois

b) Briefly explain how ONE of the remaining people would challenge the position taken by your choice in <u>part a</u>.

c) In the mid-twentieth century, the Supreme Court led the way to greater civil rights for African-Americans. Briefly explain ONE court case that best represents the court's leadership role in this endeavor.

Lesson 25

Monetary Policy—Gold vs. Silver, 1862-1900

The economic history of the United States from 1862-1900 focuses primarily on the debate over which type of currency should be in circulation: gold or silver. The question turned on whether gold would be the only medium of exchange, and if it provided for widespread economic growth and prosperity. Among eastern bankers and creditors, the answer was a resounding "yes" to "sound money," which gold represented. For farmers and other debtors however, gold was inadequate for the needs of the country and represented class oppression and exploitation.

At first the debate centered on adding paper money to gold as the basis for the currency. Later, after the Depressions of 1873 and 1893 rocked the nation, the cry for "free silver" arose. With farm prices in decline, farmers and debtors demanded that the money supply be expanded, and that silver be coined with gold at a ratio of 16 to 1. Farmers created the Populist Party in the 1890s to promote the coinage of silver, because they believed the resulting inflation would benefit them and improve their lives.

The chart on the next page analyzes many of the acts that informed this currency debate. As you review the chart, think about why the debtors/farmers were unable to convince a majority of the electorate to support their cause. Also evaluate whether "free silver" would have actually solved the agrarian problems in the last quarter of the nineteenth century.

Directions: Analyze the chart on monetary policy, and then answer the following questions.

1. Indebted farmers in the years 1862–1900 believed their greatest financial benefit would come from the
   (A) Coinage Act of 1873
   (B) Resumption Act of 1875
   (C) Gold Standard Act of 1900
   (D) Sherman Silver Purchase Act of 1890

2. "Sound money is the only basis for true economic prosperity and gold is the only real money for the United States."

   Which of the following groups would most likely agree with this statement?
   (A) supporters of the Resumption Act of 1875
   (B) supporters of the Populist Party
   (C) supporters of the Greenback-Labor Party
   (D) supporters of the Legal Tender Act of 1862

3. The "Crime of '73" occurred when
   (A) paper money was printed to supplement gold
   (B) bad money drove good money out of circulation
   (C) the use of gold caused the Depression of 1873
   (D) Congress legislated an end to minting silver coins

Monetary Policy

Act	Background	Terms	Political Impact
Legal Tender Act, 1862	As Civil War dragged on, the North was running out of money Passed to help fund the Civil War	Government authorized to print greenback dollars without species backing ($450 million)	Democrats in minority; Republicans pushed the bill through
Coinage Act, 1873	1830-1850, price of silver increased; silver became less and less available for minting 1850s, Congress discontinued silver coins; no real outcry	Demonetization Act Congress decreed silver coins should no longer be minted	Depression of 1873 hits; farmers decried the "Crime of '73" Saw conspiracy by "gold bugs" Demand for "free silver" began
Resumption Act, 1875	Union had printed $450 millions in paper money Fear "soft money" would drive "sound money" out of use	Greenbacks would be redeemed for species Gradually reduced the greenbacks in circulation	Formation of the Greenback party; later called Greenback Labor Demanded repeal of Resumption Act
Bland-Allison Act, 1878	Meant to placate 3rd party demands to expand currency Attempt to stimulate economy from Depression of 1873. Respond to pressure from farmers/miners	Treasury would buy $2–$4 million of silver each month Treasury would coin silver dollars	President Hayes' veto overridden Government purchased/minted minimum amounts of silver Neither party strongly favored act
Sherman Silver Purchase Act, 1890	Response to pressure from 3rd parties Doubled silver purchases under Bland-Allison Act Panic of 1893 caused its repeal	Government purchased 4.5 million ounces of silver monthly Issued certificates redeemable in gold or silver	Republicans supported bill; in turn, Democrats supported McKinley Tariff Populist Party and free silver were on the horizon
Gold Standard Act, 1900	Election of 1896 killed "free silver" Strikes around world increased gold supply Economic recovery lessened cry for silver	All paper money backed by gold Put U.S. on gold standard	Pinnacle of monetary conservatism Bimetalism dead as a political issue

Source Activities

Directions: Using the excerpt below and your knowledge of American history, answer the following questions.

> "Men having a design to injure business by making money scarce, could not easily get hold of all the silver, and hide it away; as they could gold… it [silver] was called the people's money. …Gold was considered the money of the rich. It was owned principally by that class of people, and the poor people seldom handled it, and the very poor people seldom saw any of it…
>
> You increase the value of all property by adding to the number of monetary units in the land. You make it possible for the debtor to pay his debts; business to start anew and revivify all the industries of the country…The money lenders in the United States, who own substantially all our money, have a selfish interest in maintaining the gold standard…"
>
> —William J. "Coins" Harvey, *Coin's Financial School*, 1894

Multiple-Choice

1. The passage above was likely written in response to a government decision to
   (A) replace species with paper currency
   (B) promote a bimentalist policy for the economy
   (C) expand the money supply by coining silver dollars
   (D) contract the money supply

2. Which of the following nineteenth-century debates most closely paralleled the controversy raised in the passage?
   (A) differences over protective tariffs in the 1820s
   (B) differences over banking and finance in the 1830s
   (C) differences over the creation of banking trusts in the 1880s
   (D) differences over the economic value of slavery in the 1850s

Short-Answer

Using the excerpt, answer parts a and b.

a) Briefly explain how TWO of the following individuals would react to the sentiments expressed in the passage:
- William Jennings Bryan
- James B. Weaver
- Grover Cleveland

b) Briefly explain how the remaining choice would react to the ideas expressed by the two individuals selected in <u>part a</u>.

Lesson 26

Social Darwinism vs. the Social Gospel Movement

The last quarter of the nineteenth century featured an intellectual struggle over the economic and moral responsibilities of the government to its citizens. On the one side were the Social Darwinists, who transformed the theory of natural selection into a survival of the fittest doctrine that explained human relationships. Citing evolutionary principles, the Social Darwinists defended the growing wealth of the upper classes, warned against government economic interference, and called for little or no direct help for the poor and disadvantaged.

On the other hand, supporters of the Social Gospel movement believed that Christianity could be an engine of social and economic reform. They saw society evolving positively, with salvation, personal growth, and social justice as possible outcomes. Centered primarily in the Protestant churches, they called for government action to alleviate poverty, combat child labor, and promote economic competition. Many of their ideas would provide the foundation for the progressive reforms from 1900–1917.

The chart on the following page compares and contrasts the two schools of thought. As you review it, think about how one group tended to look back, while the other group looked forward in terms of economic and social development in the United States. Also, consider how the ideas of the Social Darwinists influenced American overseas relations at the turn of the century.

Directions: Analyze the chart on Social Darwinists and the Social Gospel movement, and then answer the following questions.

1. Which of the following would a Social Darwinist most strongly support?
   - (A) settlement houses for immigrants
   - (B) taxes on luxury items
   - (C) creation of industrial trusts
   - (D) child labor laws

2. Which of the following statements would a supporter of the Social Gospel movement make?
   - (A) "What would Jesus do about poverty?"
   - (B) "The rich deserve their worldly rewards."
   - (C) "No man should eat the bread he has not earned."
   - (D) "Darwin's ideas have no place in human society."

3. Supporters of Social Darwinism and the Social Gospel both embraced the ideas of
   - (A) William Graham Sumner
   - (B) Washington Gladden
   - (C) Herbert Spencer
   - (D) Charles Darwin

	Social Darwinism	Social Gospel Movement
Precursors of Movement	Charles Darwin Herbert Spencer Thomas Malthus	Charles Darwin Richard Ely Lester Ward
Leading Spokesmen	William Graham Sumner Josiah Strong (Imperialism)	Walter Rauschenbusch Washington Gladden Lyman Abbot Josiah Strong (domestic issues)
Influential Literature	Darwin's *On the Origin of Species* Sumner's *Folkways* Spencer's *Principles of Biology*	Darwin's *On the Origin of Species* Rauschenbush's *Christianity and the Social Crisis* Ward's *Dynamic Sociology*
Impact of Darwin	Both ideologies used Darwin's ideas Natural selection becomes survival of the fittest (Herbert Spencer) Humans, like other life forms, struggle for survival Economic life controlled by natural law	Both ideologies used Darwin's ideas Survival of fittest is not the highest law of civilized society Organic evolution leads to better society Evolution: God's way of doing things
Ideas of Movement	Accumulation of wealth is an index of society's improvement and health Classes do not owe each other anything Competition is the law of nature Government should protect property not upset the social arrangement of nature Poverty is result of struggle for existence "Stateways cannot make folkways" (Sumner) "The world owes no man a living" (Rockefeller)	Humans can direct evolution Humans should create a "Kingdom of God" on earth Religion must play a role in public life Churches speak for those without a voice Government action is necessary in society Christian ethics can be applied to social problems Individuals must improve society Cooperation not competition to promote progress
Supporters	Industrialists: John D. Rockefeller, Andrew Carnegie Upper classes "The Forgotten Man;" tax paying, middle class Some imperialists	Protestant ministers and their congregations The poor Social activist and reformers Some advocates of Socialism
Significance	Promoted *status quo/laissez-faire* Defended the industrialists of 1880s/1890s Basis for Imperialism and unchecked Capitalism Promoted a "negative" definition of freedom Basis for the eugenics and scientific racism of the twentieth century	Justified a more active government in economic matters Addressed moral roots of social injustice Basis for "Christian Socialism" later on Influenced progressive reforms (child labor laws, settlement house movement) Supported labor union movement

Source Activities

Directions: Using the excerpt below and your knowledge of American history, answer the following questions.

> "There is a beautiful notion afloat in our literature and in the minds of our people that men are born to certain "natural rights"…In its widest extension it comes to mean that if any man finds himself uncomfortable in this world, it must be somebody else's fault, and that somebody is bound to come and make him comfortable.
>
> …Consequently the doctrine…turns out to be in practice only a scheme for making injustice prevail in human society by reversing the distribution of rewards and punishment between those who have done their duty and those who have not. …The real victim is the Forgotten Man again—the man who has watched his own investments, made his own machinery safe, …it is all wrong to preach to the Forgotten Man that it is his duty to go and remedy other people's neglect. It is not his duty…any reconstruction of society on the plan of some enthusiastic social architect…is only repeating the old error over again, …"
>
> —William Graham Sumner, "What Social Classes Owe to Each Other," 1883

Multiple-Choice

1. The ideas expressed in the passage above most clearly reflect the influence of which of the following?
   - (A) beliefs in Biblical calls for protection of the weak
   - (B) government programs to regulate working conditions
   - (C) justifications for industrial and financial consolidations
   - (D) proposals for state ownership of public utilities

2. The sentiments expressed in the passage led most directly to the twentieth-century debate over
   - (A) the proper role of government in society
   - (B) the proper role of tariffs in protecting businesses
   - (C) the proper role of the family in protecting children
   - (D) the proper role of the Constitution in regulating religious matters

Short-Answer

Using the excerpt, answer parts a and b.

a) Explain briefly how TWO of the following actions challenged American identity as it was expressed in the passage:
- The Keating Owen Act
- The Hepburn Act
- The Pure Food and Drug Act

b) Briefly explain ONE important social or political response to the needs of the "Forgotten Man" in the period from 1920 to 1970.

Lesson 27

Black Leaders, 1880–1968

As the idealism of the Reconstruction era faded during the mid-1870s, black Americans confronted a betrayal of the promise of equal rights. Increasingly the federal government's support retreated, and whites in both the South and North became more hostile toward former slaves and free blacks. As the twentieth century dawned, the shadow of Jim Crow extended across the national landscape.

By the mid-1890s, black leaders stepped forward to offer guidance in dealing with the questions of the "color line" that divided America. Some leaders suggested accommodation and integration, while others demanded a more confrontational approach in dealing with racial inequalities in America.

The chart on the following page outlines the contribution of five black leaders. As you study the chart, which leaders do you think were most constructive in their approach to the racial problems of their times, and which leaders do you think acted out of frustration and anger?

Directions: Analyze the chart on five black leaders, and then answer the following questions.

1. Booker T. Washington and Marcus Garvey shared a common belief that

    (A) alliances with liberal whites would improve civil rights for blacks

    (B) blacks should concentrate on economic progress to move toward equality

    (C) the only path to full equality is agitation and confrontation

    (D) violence was a likely outcome in the struggle for equality

2. Martin Luther King Jr. could not accept Malcolm X's policy of

    (A) striving to improve the lives of black Americans

    (B) agitation and challenge to the racial status quo

    (C) emphasizing black pride and achievements

    (D) rejecting integration and white help

3. W.E.B. Du Bois expected most of his supporters to be

    (A) black middle-class professionals

    (B) southern black sharecroppers

    (C) black urban youth

    (D) African businessmen

Influential Black Leaders

	Message	Supporters	Methods	Significance
Booker T. Washington, 1856–1915	Atlanta Compromise Accept social/political inequality Work for economic equality in farming/trades Blacks should learn vocational skills	Southern, rural blacks Southern whites Wealthy, white industrialists	Accommodation with whites Created Tuskegee Institute Blacks/whites remain separate socially Emphasized black economic development	Got money for black schools Advised presidents on racial issues Secretly tried to overturn segregation Battled NAACP/W.E.B. Du Bois
W.E.B. Du Bois, 1868–1963	Talented tenth of the black community must lead for equality Strive for full and immediate equality, including full suffrage	Intellectuals Black professionals Urban, northern blacks White progressives	Founded Niagara Movement in 1905 Helped form NAACP in 1909 Wrote books to energize blacks	Challenged B.T. Washington Agitated for equality Challenged conservative racial policies
Marcus Garvey, 1887–1940	Black self-sufficiency Opposed integration Black pride in African heritage/seek roots in Africa Proposed a "Back-to-Africa" movement Expand black economic power	Urban blacks Some whites who supported segregation of the races	Created Universal Negro Improvement Association Formed Black Star Line, a black-owned shipping company Tried to establish African economic ties	First leader to base much of his program on ties to Africa Reached many urban, northern blacks Arrested for mail fraud, deported
Malcolm X (Little), 1925–1965	Black power Enemy is white man Supported Black Nationalism May have been less separatist, more moderate at end of his life	Northern urban black youth Nation of Islam Northern white student radicals	Militant speeches, confrontations with white establishment Challenged King's nonviolence Urged self-defense against white violence	Black Muslims identified with violence in 1960s Opposed gradualism, accommodation Created an intimidating persona that whites found frightening Assassinated 1965
Martin Luther King Jr., 1929–1968	Justice by religious, moral, peaceful means Whites must see injustices in Jim Crow Later targeted economic inequality	Rural, southern church-going people White northern liberals	Nonviolent protest Marches, demonstrations Speeches, articles, books	Opened eyes of country to immorality of segregation Great moral leader Assassinated 1968

Source Activities

Directions: Using the excerpt below and your knowledge of American history, answer the following questions.

> "The political philosophy of Black Nationalism means: we must control the politics and the politicians of our community. They must no longer take orders from outside forces. We will organize, and sweep out of office all Negro politicians who are puppets for the outside forces...Whites can help us, but they can't join us. There can be no black-white unity until there is first black unity...We cannot think of uniting with others, until after we have first united among ourselves...
>
> Concerning nonviolence: it is criminal to teach a man not to defend himself when he is the constant victim of brutal attacks. It is legal and lawful to own a shotgun or a rifle. We believe in obeying the law...We should be peaceful, law-abiding—but the time has come for the American Negro to fight back in self-defense whenever and wherever he is being unjustly and unlawfully attacked."
>
> —Malcolm X, press conference, March 12, 1964

Multiple-Choice

1. Which of the following individuals from the nineteenth century most closely advocated the ideas expressed in the passage?
   - (A) William Lloyd Garrison in *The Liberator* newspaper
   - (B) David Walker in *An Appeal to the Coloured* [sic] *Citizens of the World*
   - (C) Frederick Douglass in *The North Star* newspaper
   - (D) Harriet Beecher Stowe in *Uncle Tom's Cabin*

2. The sentiment expressed in the passage most directly contributed in developing which of the following?
   - (A) the judicial rulings of the Supreme Court in the 1960s
   - (B) President Lyndon Johnson's Civil Rights program in the 1960s
   - (C) Martin Luther King Jr.'s racial beliefs in the 1960s
   - (D) the Black Power movement in the 1960s

Short-Answer

Using the excerpt, answer parts a, b, and c.

a) Briefly summarize the main points of the passage.

b) Briefly explain ONE development in the United States from 1945-1965 that led to the point of view expressed by Malcolm X.

c) Briefly explain ONE action, not mentioned in the passage, that Malcolm X hoped would transform African Americans' views of themselves and their place in American society in the mid-1960s.

Lesson 27: Black Leaders, 1880-1968

Lesson 28

The Supreme Court and Government Regulation, 1890-1937

After the Civil War, business trusts and holding companies formed. These combinations dominated the economy and abused competitors and consumers alike. In response to a public outcry for action, Congress passed the Sherman Anti-Trust Act in 1890. Although designed to reign in the power of monopolies, the act was used sparingly (18 times) from 1890–1901. Moreover, the Supreme Court, with its early twentieth-century rulings, contributed to the Act's ineffectiveness with a vague interpretation of what was meant by "combination...in restraint of trade or commerce."

From 1890–1937, the Court confronted the continuing question of whether government regulations of business under the Sherman Act went too far and infringed on the commerce clause, the general welfare clause, and the 5th/14th Amendments. Conservatives argued that the Constitution protected liberty of contracts and clearly differentiated between interstate and intrastate commerce. While reformers asked the Court to uphold laws that expanded interstate commerce, established minimum wages, and restrained child labor. Although the Court tended to support the conservative position in most cases, it also recognized some regulation of businesses, especially when government action protected women.

The following chart outlines eight of the landmark Supreme Court cases concerning the role of government in the economy from 1895–1937. As you study the cases, think about the political climate in which each case was decided, and why the intent of Congress was not always translated into Supreme Court rulings.

Directions: Analyze the chart on impactful Supreme Court cases on the role of government, and then answer the following questions.

1. Owners of trusts would be most supportive of which of the following court decisions?
   - (A) *Lochner v. New York*
   - (B) *Northern Securities v. U.S.*
   - (C) *Muller v. Oregon*
   - (D) *West Coast Hotel Co. v. Parrish*

2. The court case that provided the greatest encouragement to supporters of government regulation of the economy was:
   - (A) *U.S. v. E.C. Knight*
   - (B) *Lochner v. New York*
   - (C) *Northern Securities v. U.S.*
   - (D) *Adkins v. Children's Hospital*

3. When deciding the constitutionality of various state and federal regulations the Court often considered whether a law
   - (A) expanded opportunities for minorities
   - (B) expanded the economy and jobs
   - (C) violated the 2nd Amendment
   - (D) violated liberty of contract protection

Threads of History

Case	Issue Raised	Ruling	Significance
U.S. v. E.C. Knight Co., 1895	Was Sherman Act constitutional? Was manufacturing a part of commerce?	Act was constitutional. Manufacturing precedes commerce—E.C. Knight Co. did not violate Sherman Act	Limited definition of commerce and the reach of Sherman Act. States should regulate manufacturing
Northern Securities Co. v. U.S., 1904	Did Sherman Act apply to holding companies like J.P. Morgan had assembled?	Holding companies were covered by Act. Morgan's Company did restrain trade	Gave energy to trust busting. Temporarily curtailed merging of companies
Lochner v. New York, 1905	Did New York's restriction of baker's hours violate liberty of contracts in Constitution?	NY law exceeded state's police power. State unreasonably interfered with right of contract	Established "Lochner Era" of judicial veto of much regulation. Ruling used to restrict government actions for next 32 years
Muller v. Oregon, 1908	Did restriction of women's hours violate 14th Amendment? Were women in a "special physical" class?	Restriction constitutional. State's police power protected women's physical and maternal function	Established "Brandeis brief" using sociological and medical evidence. Did not overturn Lochner, but women deemed a special exception
Standard Oil v. U.S., 1911	Did Rockefeller's Standard Oil Company violate the Sherman Act?	Company represented an "unreasonable" restraint of trade. Company must be broken up	Established "rule of reason," a precedent that lasted for many years. Added to uncertainty over Sherman Act
Adkins v. Children's Hospital, 1923	Did federal minimum wage for women violate the due process clause in 5th Amendment?	Act did violate liberty of contracts. Women could not be restricted anymore than men in marketplace	Overturned Muller. Nineteenth Amendment had eliminated women's special status. Ruling overturned in 1937
Schechter Poultry Corp. v. U.S., 1935	Did National Industrial Recovery Act (NIRA) violate commerce/general welfare clauses of Constitution?	NIRA unconstitutional. Delegated legislative power to executive. Violated commerce clause	Message to FDR: economic crisis did allow excessive government actions. Played a role in FDR's court packing decision in 1937
West Coast Hotel Co. v. Parrish, 1937	Did Washington state's minimum wage law for women violate liberty of contracts protected by 5th and 14th Amendments?	Law constitutional. State could regulate for public interest. Law protected community/safety of vulnerable group	Overturned Adkins. Ended "Lochner Era." Some said reaction to court packing—"switch in time that saved nine"

Lesson 28: The Supreme Court and Government Regulation

Source Activities

Directions: Using the excerpts below and your knowledge of American history, answer the following questions.

"The statute necessarily interferes with the right of contract between the employer and employees, concerning the number of hours in which the latter may labor in the bakery of the employer. The general right to make a contract in relation to his business is part of the liberty of the individual protected by the 14th Amendment of the Federal Constitution…

The act…is an illegal interference with the rights of individuals, both employers and employees, to make contracts regarding labor upon such terms as they may think best, or they may agree upon with other parties to such contracts…"

—*Lochner v. New York*, 1905

"The single question is the constitutionality of the statue under which the defendant was convicted so far as affects the work of a female in a laundry. …That woman's physical structure and the performance of maternal functions place her at a disadvantage in the struggle for subsistence is obvious. This is especially true when the burdens of motherhood are upon her…

Differentiated by these matters from the other sex, she is properly placed in a class by herself, and legislations designed for her protection may be sustained even when the legislation is not necessary for men…The limitations which this statute places upon her contractual powers, upon her right to agree with her employer as to the time she shall labor, are not solely for her benefit, but also largely for the benefit of all…we are of the opinion that it cannot be adjudged that the act in question is in conflict with the federal Constitution…"

—*Muller v. Oregon*, 1908

Multiple-Choice

1. The two excerpts best serve as evidence that the Supreme Court of the early twentieth century believed
   - (A) that the federal government should not intervene in the workplace
   - (B) that all workers must be treated equally in the workplace
   - (C) that women were better workers than men in the workplace
   - (D) that men and women had different rights in the workplace

2. Which of the following twentieth-century continuities most resembles the struggle over individual versus corporate property rights?
   - (A) attempts to expand government power in the 1930s
   - (B) attempts to expand economic rights for African Americans in the 1910s
   - (C) attempts to expand gender economic rights in the 1960s
   - (D) attempts to deregulate industries in the 1980s

Short-Answer

Using the excerpts, answer parts a and b.

a) Briefly explain how TWO of the following groups would react to the excerpted court decisions:
   - Members of the National Woman's Party
   - Members of the Bull Moose Party
   - Members of the Industrial Workers of the World

b) The two Court decisions excerpted made a statement about American identity in the early twentieth century. Briefly explain how ONE of the following Supreme Court decisions helps define American identity later in the century:
   - *Korematsu v. U.S.*
   - *Brown v. Board of Education*
   - *Roe v. Wade*

Lesson 29

Reform Movements of the Twentieth Century

The great domestic political struggle of twentieth-century American history occurred between the impulses of reform and the forces of the status quo. A major issue in this debate was the degree to which the national government should involve itself in the social and economic lives of its citizens—the issue of *laissez-faire*. This conflict over government intervention into the private sector defined the major domestic political and economic debate during most of the twentieth century.

Reformers made three major attempts to alter American social and economic relations during the twentieth century: the progressive reforms early in the century; the New Deal/Fair Deal reforms of the 1930s and 1940s; and the New Frontier/Great Society reforms of the 1960s. The chart on the following page summarizes each of the movements. Historians have noted that these reforms occurred in roughly thirty-year cycles during the twentieth century. That is, a wave of public purpose (reform) was usually followed by a private interlude (i.e., 1920s, 1950s, and 1980s). What factors might explain this cycle of reform?

Directions: Analyze the chart on the three twentieth-century reform movements, and then answer the following questions.

1. A common thread that ran through the Fair Deal, New Frontier, and Great Society was

   (A) each was led by a Republican president
   (B) each occurred after the United States completed a successful war
   (C) each tried to continue and expand New Deal reforms
   (D) each relied on state governments to make societal changes

2. Which pair of twentieth-century reform movements was most effective in changing America?

   (A) The New Deal and the Great Society
   (B) The Great Society and the New Frontier
   (C) The New Deal and the Fair Deal
   (D) The Square Deal/New Freedom and the Great Society

3. In terms of actual accomplishments, which of these reform programs had the least impact on American society?

   (A) New Deal
   (B) New Frontier
   (C) Fair Deal
   (D) Great Society

120 – *Threads of History*

Twentieth-Century Reform Movements

	Square Deal/ New Freedom	New Deal	Fair Deal	New Frontier	Great Society
Dates	1901–1916	1933–1939	1945–1953	1961–1963	1963–1969
Leader(s)	T. Roosevelt W. Wilson	F. Roosevelt	H. Truman	J. Kennedy	L. Johnson
Goals	Control corporations, trusts Citizen protection Clean up government Conserve environment	Relief for unemployed Recovery from the Depression Reform of financial institutions, economic system	Continue/expand New Deal with special attention to economic security	Continue/expand New Deal with some attention to civil rights, education	Complete New Deal with special attention to poverty, cities, civil rights, healthcare, education
Actions	Hepburn Act Pure Food and Drug Act Clayton Act Northern Securities Case Federal Reserve Act Federal Trade Commission Newlands Act Keating-Owen Act Progressive Amendments (16th, 17th)	National Industrial Recovery Act Agricultural Adjustment Act Civilian Conservation Corp Public Works Administration Social Security Act Federal Deposit Insurance Corporation Tennessee Valley Authority Securities and Exchange Commission Wagner Act	Desegregated military Employment Act 1946 Raised minimum wage Expanded Social Security Proposed civil rights program	Proposed: • Medicare • Civil Rights Act • Aid to education • Public housing • Mass transit	Medicare/Medicaid Act Civil Rights Act Voting Rights Act 60 education acts Economic Opportunity Act Housing Act Immigration Act Highway Safety Act Head Start program Model Cities Act

Lesson 29: Reform Movements of the 20th Century

Source Activities

Directions: Using the excerpt below and your knowledge of American history, answer the following questions.

> "I have called for a national war on poverty. Our objective: total victory.
>
> There are millions of Americans—one fifth of our people—who have not shared in the abundance which has been granted to most of us, and on whom the gates of opportunity have been closed. ...The war on poverty is not a struggle simply to support people, to make them dependent on the generosity of others...
>
> It is an effort to allow them to develop and use their capacities, as we have been allowed to develop and use ours, so that they can share, as others share, in the promise of the nation.
>
> Our history has proved that each time we broaden the base of abundance, giving more people the chance to produce and consume, we create new industry, higher production, increased earnings and better income for all. ...Because it is right, because it is wise, and because for the first time in our history, it is possible to conquer poverty, I submit for the consideration of the Congress and the country, the Economic Opportunity Act of 1964."
>
> —President Lyndon B. Johnson, 1964

Multiple-Choice

1. Which of the following activities from the early years of the twentieth century most closely resembled President Johnson's call for action in the passage?
   - (A) governmental promotion of high tariffs on imported goods
   - (B) governmental expansion of suffrage in the United States
   - (C) governmental regulation of working hours for women
   - (D) governmental calls for private donations to help the poor

2. Which of the following controversies in the 1980s arose most directly from the sentiment expressed in the passage above?
   - (A) a debate over the amount of government spending on social programs
   - (B) a debate over whether whites and blacks should receive government help
   - (C) a debate over federal versus state regulation of corporations
   - (D) a debate over government aid to parochial schools

29

Short-Answer

Using the excerpt, answer parts a, b, and c.

a) Briefly explain how ONE of the following movements sought to change the federal government's role in the social and economic life of the nation:
- The New Deal
- The Fair Deal
- The Great Society

b) In both the early twentieth century and the 1960s, the federal government attempted to address the question of poverty and social justice. Briefly explain ONE important similarity in the reasons why this spirit of reform emerged in both time periods.

c) Provide ONE piece of evidence from the 1960s, that is not included in the passage, and explain how it supported President Johnson's message.

Lesson 29: Reform Movements of the 20th Century

Lesson 30

Isolationism vs. Internationalism, 1919–1941

Between the two World Wars, isolationists and internationalists struggled over what role America should play in the military and political affairs of Europe. Both sides realized the United States could not withdraw from world affairs completely, yet the isolationists consistently opposed membership in the League of Nations and the World Court. They did, however, support multilateral disarmament treaties that saved taxes, reduced the power of the federal government, and, theoretically, the chances of war.

The onset of the Great Depression strengthened the isolationists' (noninterventionists) hand. The nation, preoccupied with economic problems during this time, accepted a series of Neutrality Acts that reinforced its nonentangling, foreign policy stance. When Germany invaded Poland in September 1939, however, public opinion shifted toward the internationalist position. Between 1939 and America's entry into the war in 1941, President Roosevelt gradually sought more aid for, and involvement with, potential European allies, such as Great Britain.

The chart on the following page compares the two contrasting viewpoints from 1919 to 1941. Do you think Roosevelt was too timid in his approach to foreign relations during the 1930s? Why is the label "isolationism" somewhat inaccurate during these years?

Directions: Analyze the chart on internationalism and isolationism, and then answer the following questions.

1. The issue that divided the isolationists and internationalists most deeply immediately after the Great War (World War I) was whether the United States should
   (A) make a permanent alliance with Great Britain
   (B) reduce spending on the military
   (C) raise taxes to support foreign aid
   (D) accept membership in the League of Nations

2. Between 1919–1941, William Borah, Charles Lindbergh, and Gerald Nye all shared the belief that
   (A) the U.S. should cease trading with most nations in the world
   (B) European alliances would make America safer
   (C) England's security was vital to America's security
   (D) America should avoid involving itself in European politics

3. Internationalists between 1919 and 1941 strongly believed in
   (A) nonentangling foreign alliances
   (B) collective security
   (C) reducing military spending
   (D) disarmament and immigration restriction

Comparing Internationalists and Isolationists

	Internationalists	Isolationists
Principles	Collective security U.S. had interest in European security Confront overseas aggression Axis powers a threat to U.S. Quarantine aggressors British and American security linked Atlantic Charter	Avoid entangling foreign alliances Great War a mistake Arms makers had manipulated U.S. into Great War Avoid defending England's interests Reduce military Keep taxes low Domestic issues more important than foreign affairs Defend continental U.S.
Actions	Should accept Article 10 Should join League of Nations Should join World Court Stimson Doctrine Reciprocal trade agreements Offer aid short of war Provide lend-lease	Alter/reject Article 10 Reject League of Nations Reject membership in World Court Washington Naval agreement Kellogg-Briand Pact Immigration restrictions Hawley-Smoot tariff Nye munitions investigation Neutrality Acts 1935, 1936, 1937
Personnel	Woodrow Wilson Franklin Roosevelt Cordell Hull Henry Stimson Frank Knox Tom Connally Committee to Defend America	Henry Cabot Lodge William Borah Gerald Nye Charles Lindbergh Hiram Johnson Robert Taft America First Committee
Comments	Reeling during 1920s from League of Nations' defeat In 1930s, first priority was economic recovery No European support against Axis Roosevelt unwilling to challenge isolationists in Congress When France fell in June of 1940, the internationalists gained political strength	Sought economic internationalism Avoid political/military overseas connections Keep America's freedom of action abroad Reached height with Neutrality Acts

Source Activities

Directions: Using the excerpt below and your knowledge of American history, answer the following questions.

> "No one is more jealously interested in my country's maintaining adequate national defense than I am. But I am sick of things being done in the name of national defense. ...The serious danger to our peace, to say nothing about our standards of common honor and decency, is so obvious that a way out of the bog in which we find ourselves must be found. A policy of strict neutrality... appears to be such a way of escape...
>
> The truth is that unless a halt is called upon war preparations that are not for defense and upon the enactment of laws for the complete mobilization of our civil organization in wartime, America will succumb to war psychology and will be drawn inevitably into actual conflict...
>
> For better or worse, we are part of the world order...But let us refrain from writing the ticket of procedure even before we know who our allies are to be, what cause is to be, what the jeopardy is going to be..."
>
> —Senator Gerald P. Nye, "Is Neutrality Possible for America?" in *Tomorrow in the Making*, 1939

Multiple-Choice

1. Which of the following nineteenth-century issues raised concerns that were similar to those expressed in the passage?
    (A) tariff wars between the United States and Europe
    (B) conflicts over fishing rights in the Atlantic Ocean
    (C) armed conflicts between European countries
    (D) troubles with Spain over ownership of Florida

2. The sentiments expressed in the passage above led most directly to the 1940s controversy over
    (A) membership in the World Court
    (B) involvement in European trade agreements
    (C) sending anti-communist aid to China
    (D) membership in the North Atlantic Treaty Organization

Short-Answer

Using the excerpt, answer parts a, b, and c.

a) Briefly explain how ONE of the following foreign policy actions affected the debate over American isolationism from 1919–1941:
- The rejection of the Treaty of Versailles
- The Neutrality Acts of the mid-1930s
- The Atlantic Charter

b) United States non-involvement in Europe had a long history before the 1930s. Briefly explain ONE example of America's reluctance to entangle itself in European affairs from 1790–1825.

c) Briefly explain ONE development that challenged the sentiment expressed in the passage from 1945–1955.

Lesson 31

Transformation of Capitalism in the 1930s

The New Deal was Franklin Roosevelt's plan to restore economic prosperity to the United States during the 1930s. Though Roosevelt expanded the powers of the federal government enormously from 1933 to 1939 and alleviated the suffering of millions of Americans, his economic programs failed to end the Depression. It would take the Second World War to accomplish that.

Roosevelt's program to alleviate the Depression had two distinct phases. A First New Deal from 1933 to 1935 concentrated on economic relief and recovery and attempted to establish a government partnership with American corporations and businesses. A Second New Deal from 1935–1939 focused on long-term reforms in the American economy and took a confrontational stance toward the business community and the wealthy by imposing higher taxes and new, stricter regulations.

The chart on the next page outlines the basic differences between the First and Second New Deals. As you study it, consider the factors that undermined cooperation between big business and the government. Further, in what ways did the First and Second New Deals attempt to alter the capitalist system?

Directions: Analyze the chart on the First and Second New Deals, and then answer the following questions.

1. During the First New Deal, Franklin Roosevelt believed
   (A) the National Recovery Administration should nationalize the major industries
   (B) corporations that provided public services must accept government regulations and limitations on their profits
   (C) businessmen should be left alone to make as much money as possible
   (D) the government must cooperate with the business community to lift the country out of the Depression

2. In the Second New Deal, the government's attitude toward wealthy Americans was that
   (A) the gap between the wealthy and other classes should be narrowed through taxing policy
   (B) rich people should be protected because their spending could stimulate prosperity
   (C) the incomes of all Americans should be roughly equal
   (D) inherited wealth hurt the country and prolonged the depression

3. The primary goal of the First New Deal was
   (A) to control all aspects of the American economic system
   (B) to provide relief and recovery from the Depression
   (C) to break up the trusts that had formed since the Progressive era
   (D) to establish cooperative ownership of America's farms and businesses

Comparing the First and Second New Deals

	First New Deal	Second New Deal
Dates	1933–1935	1935–1939
Goals	Direct relief to unemployed; recovery from the Depression Cooperated with business community to restore pre-1929 prosperity Helped organized labor to improve position in society Provided assistance to agriculture	Revived progressive tradition of trust regulation Strengthened organized labor Sought to meet needs of workers, elderly, disabled, farmers, unemployed Narrowed class differences by taxing the wealthy Supported industrial workers and small farmers
Position on Business	Partnership Cooperation Suspended antitrust actions	Confrontational toward corporate interests Strong regulation of public utilities
Actions	National Industrial Recovery Act Agricultural Adjustment Act Federal Emergency Relief Act Emergency Banking Act Civilian Conservation Corp Tennessee Valley Authority Act	Public Utility Holding Company Act Wealth Tax Act (Revenue Act) National Labor Relations Act (Wagner Act) Works Progress Administration Social Security Act Fair Labor Standards Act
Comments	Brief honeymoon between business community and the Roosevelt administration First New Deal told business what it must do Business found New Deal regulations increasingly confining and intrusive Supreme Court sided with business interests as it struck down several major New Deal acts	Stronger controls and higher taxes on the wealthy and large businesses Responded to attacks by Liberty League and Supreme Court's judicial review Second New Deal told business what it must *not* do

Source Activities

Directions: Using the cartoon below and your knowledge of American history, answer the following questions.

The Washington Star, June 2, 1935

Multiple-Choice

1. The ideas expressed in the cartoon most directly reflect which of the following continuities in United States history?
   - (A) debates over the role of the federal government in economic matters
   - (B) debates over the transportation system that best suited the nation
   - (C) debates over presidential power to amend the Constitution
   - (D) debates over the role of the federal government in religious matters

2. The question highlighted in the cartoon was raised earlier in the twentieth century when the federal government began to
   - (A) desegregate the schools in the South
   - (B) provide health care for immigrant groups
   - (C) establish a uniform currency in the United States
   - (D) regulate corporate business practices

Short-Answer

Using the cartoon, answer parts a, b, and c.

a) Briefly explain how ONE of the following individuals would react to the ideas expressed in the cartoon:
   - Harry Hopkins
   - Norman Thomas
   - Herbert Hoover

b) Briefly explain how ONE of the remaining individuals would challenge the response of the individual selected in <u>part a</u>.

c) Briefly explain ONE example of how President Roosevelt sought to implement the point of view expressed in the cartoon from 1933–1941.

Lesson 31: Transformation of Capitalism in the 1930s - 131

Lesson 32

Presidential Civil Rights Records, 1945-1974

The Second World War helped launch the civil rights movement of the 1950s and 1960s. After defeating the racist philosophy of the Axis powers, President Truman began to evaluate race relations in the United States. Influenced by African-Americans' wartime sacrifices and their mistreatment in America, the president proposed a civil rights program. Although Truman's program met opposition from his own party and Republicans in Congress, he marked the path toward greater racial justice in America.

Building on Truman's momentum, the Supreme Court issued a series of rulings that culminated in *Brown v. Board of Education* (1954), which outlawed Jim Crow in America. During the next fifteen years, leaders such as Martin Luther King Jr. and Lyndon Johnson promoted racial equality and changed the face of America.

From 1945 to 1974, presidential motives and actions on civil rights varied greatly. Most chief executives weighed the political costs before taking action on behalf of African-Americans. The chart on the next page compares the proposals and actions of the presidents from Truman to Nixon. As you study the information, which one of these five presidents would you nominate as African-Americans' greatest ally in the quest for equality?

Directions: Analyze the chart on civil rights proposals and actions, and then answer the following questions.

1. In terms of civil rights, Dwight Eisenhower and Richard Nixon shared

   (A) a desire to achieve racial equality regardless of the political costs

   (B) a desire to make civil rights a weapon in fighting the Cold War

   (C) a weak commitment toward civil rights

   (D) a belief that federal laws could change people's racial attitudes

2. For John F. Kennedy, civil rights was an issue

   (A) of the highest moral priority from the very beginning of his presidency

   (B) to be managed without political conflict within his party

   (C) to be completely ignored until it required action

   (D) to be postponed until he was re-elected

3. Lyndon Johnson's civil rights program was undermined by

   (A) opposition from liberal Democrats and the Supreme Court

   (B) budget deficits and economic recession

   (C) affirmative action and the Republican controlled Congress

   (D) domestic unrest and the war in Vietnam

Civil Rights Proposals and Actions, 1945–1974

President	Proposals	Actions	Comments
Harry Truman	Antilynching law Voter protection End discrimination in military, interstate travel, government hiring End poll tax	Created Civil Rights Committee First president to address the NAACP Desegregated the armed forces Reduced government job discrimination	Civil rights program blocked by Congress Won African Americans to Democratic Party Alienated South (Strom Thurmond's Dixiecrat revolt)
Dwight Eisenhower	Work for mildest forms of civil rights Racial justice part of Cold War struggle	Appointed Earl Warren to Supreme Court Civil Rights Acts of 1957/1960 Ended segregation in D.C. and on military bases Sent federal troops to Little Rock	Lacked conviction on civil rights Avoided compulsory action on civil rights Sought change through reason and prayer Believed government could not legislate morality
John Kennedy	Enforce existing laws End discrimination in public housing Made civil rights a moral issue in June 1963	Defended freedom riders Enforced desegregation of universities Ended public housing discrimination Proposed Civil Rights Act	Hoped to contain civil rights pressures/actions Feared southern Democrats in Congress Came late to supporting civil rights Clashed with King, wiretapped him
Lyndon Johnson	Include African-Americans in Great Society Wage war on poverty Overcome racism Improve cities and urban schools	Civil Rights Act of 1964 Voting Rights Act of 1965 Economic Opportunity Act Appointed Thurgood Marshall to Supreme Court 60 education laws, including Head Start	Greatest presidential supporter of civil rights Great Society very strong on civil rights Urban riots 1964–1968 undermined program Great Society damaged by Vietnam War
Richard Nixon	Bring nation together Restore law and order Called for extra help for urban blacks	Supported affirmative action briefly Desegregated many schools Extended Voting Rights Act Condemned busing Appointed conservative federal judges	In the past, he had a moderate record on civil rights Lacked commitment to true racial equality Used race to divide Democrats Gradually followed a southern racial strategy

Source Activities

Directions: Using the excerpt below and your knowledge of American history, answer the following questions.

> "For a few minutes this evening I want to talk to you about the serious situation that has arisen in Little Rock. …In that city, under the leadership of demagogic extremists, disorderly mobs have deliberately prevented the carrying out of proper orders from a Federal Court. Local authorities have not eliminated that violent opposition, and, under the law, I yesterday issued a Proclamation calling upon the mob to disperse.
>
> This morning the mob again gathered in front of the Central High School of Little Rock, obviously for the purpose of again preventing the carrying out of the Court's order relating to the admission of Negro children to that school. …I have today issued an Executive Order directing the use of troops under Federal authority to aid in the execution of Federal law at Little Rock, Arkansas. …Our personal opinions about the decision have no bearing on the matter of enforcement; the responsibility and authority of the Supreme Court to interpret the Constitution are very clear. …Mob rule cannot be allowed to override the decision of our courts."
>
> —President Dwight D. Eisenhower, 1957

Multiple-Choice

1. The sentiments expressed in the passage above most clearly show the influence of which of the following?
   - (A) late nineteenth-century states' rights claims to manage racial conflicts
   - (B) mid twentieth-century judicial rulings on racial conflicts
   - (C) early twentieth-century military interventions in racial conflicts
   - (D) late nineteenth-century judicial rulings on racial conflicts

2. Which of the following events in the nineteenth century most closely parallels the controversy described in the passage?
   - (A) the use of troops to end racial violence during labor strikes
   - (B) the use of troops to put down urban rioting among African Americans
   - (C) the use of troops to implement Reconstruction in the South
   - (D) the use of troops to maintain racially segregated schools in the North

Short-Answer

Using the excerpt, answer parts a, b, and c.

a) Briefly explain how ONE of the following documents influenced President Eisenhower's message in the passage:
- *Brown v. Board of Education*, 1954
- The Southern Manifesto, 1956
- "To Secure These Rights," 1947

b) The "Second Reconstruction" is a term often used by historians to mark the launching of the modern civil rights movement. Briefly explain how ONE of the documents listed in <u>part a</u> best represented the beginning of that era.

c) Briefly explain why ONE of the other options is not as useful in marking the beginning of the period as your choice in <u>part b</u>.

Lesson 33

Containment, 1945-1975

At the end of the Second World War, the tenuous wartime alliance between the United States and Soviet Union broke apart. Unable to agree over the future of Eastern Europe, the two superpowers began a nonshooting competition that columnist Walter Lippman labeled a "Cold War."

The United States' strategy in this struggle was to contain communist expansion around the world. Largely influenced by George Kennan's article "The Sources of Soviet Conduct" and his "Long Telegram," the Truman administration viewed the Soviet Union as an ideologically driven power, bent on world conquest. Faced with this enemy, Truman decided to follow the "patient, but firm and vigilant containment" of Soviet expansion. Although labeled in different ways, and focused on varying geographical regions, this policy became the foundation of United States Cold War strategy for the next thirty years.

The chart on the next page outlines how five presidents approached containment from 1945 to 1975. As you study this information, consider the following: Were there alternatives to containment? What domestic political factors influenced containment? Was the containment policy too reactive and costly?

Directions: Analyze the chart on containment, and then answer the following questions.

1. During the late 1940s, the Truman administration implemented containment by
   - (A) sending combat soldiers to repel communist attacks
   - (B) using air power and atomic bombs to stop Communism
   - (C) using China as a diplomatic tool to contain Communism
   - (D) sending economic aid to countries threatened by Communism

2. President Kennedy believed that America's containment policy should
   - (A) rely on many types of military force to block Communism
   - (B) abandon Vietnam since it was not critical to American security
   - (C) negotiate with Fidel Castro to weaken his alliance with the Soviet Union
   - (D) not be concerned about Communism in the Third World

3. President Nixon differed from his predecessors with a containment policy that
   - (A) used the CIA to spy on the Soviet Union
   - (B) sent military and economic aid to allies in Europe
   - (C) used diplomacy with China as a means of containing the Soviet Union
   - (D) relied on nuclear weapons to maintain world peace

Containment Approaches, 1945-1975

President	Strategy	Means/Implementation	Comments
Harry Truman	Containment	Used economic and military aid Sent troops where necessary Programs: • Truman Doctrine • Marshall Plan • North Atlantic Treaty Organization (NATO) Sent troops to Korea	Communist threat in Greece and Turkey required U.S. aid Sent aid to Europe 1948–1953 NATO first entangling alliance for U.S. Korean conflict—first limited war
Dwight Eisenhower	"New Look" to contain Communism	Massive retaliation Rollback of Communism Brinkmanship Used CIA to spy on, and topple communist regimes Eisenhower Doctrine in Middle East	Relied on air power, nuclear weapons Made empty pleas for freeing communist-controlled areas in Europe Take USSR to brink of nuclear war if necessary Used CIA to keep Iran, Guatemala friendly to U.S.; U-2 spy planes
John Kennedy	"Flexible response" to contain communist aggression Stand firm in Europe	Combated wars of national liberation in the Third World Used counterinsurgency forces Strong stand in Berlin Blocked Communism in Cuba, Vietnam	Berlin wall erected Used guerrilla as well as conventional forces Tried to topple Castro, but resulted in Bay of Pigs Cuban Missile Crisis brought world to brink of nuclear war Sent 16,000 troops to Vietnam
Lyndon Johnson	Containment in Asia Stand firm in Europe by maintaining NATO	Sent 500,000+ troops to Vietnam; tried for political settlement with military forces Bombed North Vietnam	Widened Vietnam War Tried to negotiate with Soviets in Europe
Richard Nixon	Vietnamization Détente Nixon Doctrine Opened China	Reduced U.S. troops in Vietnam Maintained NATO Negotiated with USSR Diplomatic agreements with China	Withdrew U.S. troops from Vietnam Kept commitments in other parts of world Used China to contain the Soviet Union Peace settlement in Vietnam

Source Activities

Directions: Using the cartoon below and your knowledge of American history, answer the following questions.

The Minneapolis Star, 1947

Multiple-Choice

1. The idea expressed in the cartoon above most directly reflected the Cold War belief that the United States should

   (A) provide medical assistance to deal with the chaos in Western Europe

   (B) accept communist domination of Western Europe

   (C) work with communist nations to preserve the peace in Western Europe

   (D) become more active in stopping Communism in Western Europe

2. The sentiments expressed in the cartoon most directly led to which of the following Cold War actions by the United States?

   (A) the extension of economic and financial aid to Europe

   (B) the creation of the World Health Organization in Europe

   (C) the use of tactical nuclear weapons in Europe

   (D) the recreation of the Grand Alliance in Europe

Short-Answer

Using the cartoon, answer parts a, b, and c.

a) Briefly explain how the beliefs expressed in the cartoon impacted ONE of the following Cold War developments:
- The creation of the Truman Doctrine, 1947
- The development of the Marshall Plan, 1947
- The establishment of the North Atlantic Treaty Organization, 1949

b) Briefly explain how the point of view expressed in the cartoon marked a major departure in American foreign policy after World War II.

c) Briefly explain ONE development in foreign affairs after 1975 that challenged the point of view of the cartoon.

Lesson 33: Containment, 1945-1975 - **139**

Lesson 34

Failure of Containment—The Vietnam War

For the United States, the Vietnam War was the most divisive and controversial conflict of the post-World War II era. It divided America internally and ended with a communist victory in South Vietnam in 1975. Initiated as a minor part of United States's postwar containment policy, aid to South Vietnam eventually grew into a full-scale American military commitment that, by the late 1960s, had become the centerpiece of American foreign policy. The Vietnam struggle was a thread that wove itself through post-World War II history from Truman to Nixon. Each administration contributed in some way to the tragedy that the war became for the United States.

The chart on the next page will help place the war in perspective and provide a review of critical information. It presents an overview of the war from the Truman years through the end of the conflict in 1975. As you study the information, identify three or four critical turning points in America's descent into the tragic quagmire of the war.

Directions: Analyze the chart on the Vietnam War, and then answer the following questions.

1. Presidents Eisenhower, Kennedy, and Johnson sent aid and troops to Vietnam because they believed
    (A) that Vietnam had been a long-term ally of the United States and deserved support
    (B) that the United States Congress supported Diem's reform policies
    (C) that Ho Chi Minh would abandon Communism if confronted by American force
    (D) that the domino theory was correct and Vietnam was critical to containing Communism

2. Lyndon Johnson escalated the war in Vietnam because he
    (A) hoped to block French colonialism in the region
    (B) feared the war's loss would hurt his domestic agenda and America's credibility in the world
    (C) believed the Soviet Union was sending thousands of troops to North Vietnam
    (D) believed U.S. assistance was the only way to maintain Ngo Dinh Diem in power

3. A critical decision made by Dwight Eisenhower in Vietnam was to
    (A) select and support Ngo Dinh Diem as an American ally
    (B) abandon the domino theory in South East Asia
    (C) send 540,000 combat soldiers to fight in Vietnam
    (D) begin bombing North Vietnam

Overview of the Vietnam War

President	Background	Actions/Events	Significance of Action
Harry Truman	1945–1949 France tried to recolonize Indochina Ho Chi Minh and communists resisted U.S. opposed French recolonization, but feared Communism	1949–1953 U.S. began massive aid to France; by 1953 was paying 80% of French bills in Indochina Sent O.S.S./C.I.A. to work with French to combat communists	Fall of China, Korean War put pressure on Truman to hold line on Communism in Asia Supported French colonialism in order to stop Communism
Dwight Eisenhower	1954, Dien Bien Phu fell; French defeated Geneva Conference divided Indochina Proposed unification elections be held in 1956	Selected Ngo Dinh Diem as U.S. ally Supported Diem's decision not to hold elections in 1956 Gave economic aid Sent 1,000 advisers to Vietnam	Domino theory made Vietnam critical to Asian containment Support of Diem laid foundation for future commitments
John Kennedy	Worried by Diem's repression of Buddhists and Diem's refusal to reform political corruption in South Viet Cong grew in strength	JFK resisted call to send combat troops Increased advisers to 16,000 Supported domino theory Tacitly supported Diem's ouster in 1963	Postponed either escalation or withdrawal No clear future direction on war Diem's death left South in political and military chaos
Lyndon Johnson	Faced political chaos in Vietnam Believed in domino theory Feared conservative political attacks on Great Society Realized fighting war could destroy his presidency	Gulf of Tonkin Resolution 1964 gave LBJ authority to fight war Began bombing North Vietnam Sent combat troops to Vietnam; by 1968, 540,000 troops in South Vietnam Opposition to war grew	Saw war as test of U.S. will as superpower Escalated the war and gradually divided nation Tet Offensive set stage for U.S. desire to withdraw from Vietnam War destroyed Johnson's presidency and tarnished his legacy
Richard Nixon (Ford)	Pledged to "Vietnamize" war Claimed he had a secret plan to end the war	Reduced U.S. role in war Invaded Cambodia Bombed North Vietnam Peace accords in 1973 left communists in South Vietnam	Ended draft; withdrew U.S. troops Watergate removed Nixon and reduced public support for South Vietnam Communists took over South Vietnam in 1975

Lesson 34: Failure of Containment—The Vietnam War

Source Activities

Directions: Using the photograph below and your knowledge of American history, answer the following questions.

Veterans for Peace rally, San Francisco, 1969

Multiple-Choice

1. The action in the photograph reflects most directly on which of the following continuities in United States history?

   (A) the debate over using public property for private protests in wartime

   (B) the debate over who should be allowed to protest in wartime

   (C) the debate over military service in wartime

   (D) the debate over the Constitutional limits of protest in wartime

2. The controversy expressed in the photograph most directly contributed to which of the following developments in the 1960s and 1970s?

   (A) frustration and anger over unemployment among minorities

   (B) boycotts of goods produced by defense contractors

   (C) conflict and turmoil within the political parties

   (D) conflict over the ending of student draft deferments

142 - *Threads of History*

Short-Answer

Using the photograph, answer parts a, b, and c.

a) Briefly explain how ONE of the following individuals would react to the point of view expressed in the photograph:
- A member of the Student Non-Violent Coordinating Committee
- A member of Students for a Democratic Society
- A member of a World War II veterans organization

b) Briefly explain how ONE of the remaining individuals would react to the point of view expressed in your answer to <u>part a</u>.

c) There is a long tradition of Americans protesting United States involvement in armed conflicts. Briefly explain ONE instance, besides the one depicted in the photograph, of domestic opposition to America's warfare against another nation.

Lesson 35

Famous Doctrines— from Monroe to Nixon

On several occasions in American history, presidents have unilaterally asserted American intentions in various parts of the world. These presidential doctrines have been issued without the force of either treaty or international agreement. Yet, because they have coincided with American interests in the region, they have been accepted by the American people, supported by Congress, and heeded by the international community. In all cases, the doctrines were only assertions by presidents and their foreign policy advisers of America's goals and desires in specific regions of the world. Other nations have usually acquiesced to the doctrines because of America's power and position in the regions affected by the pronouncements.

The chart on the next page outlines the four major doctrines in U.S. history. As you study the information, consider under what authority America made its decrees about other parts of the world. Did the United States possess the moral right to tell the rest of the world what to do? Also, were the doctrines merely reflections of American self-interest or did they serve international peace and order?

Directions: Analyze the chart on four famous doctrines in American history, and then answer the following questions.

1. One of the objectives of the Truman and Eisenhower Doctrines was to
   (A) save China from Communism
   (B) oust Fidel Castro from Cuba
   (C) conserve American foreign aid and money
   (D) contain communist expansion

2. The principal goal of the Monroe Doctrine was to
   (A) warn Europe against colonizing in the Western Hemisphere
   (B) prevent the seizure of American shipping during European wars
   (C) stop Britain from impressing U.S. sailors
   (D) block the spread of democracy in South America

3. The Nixon Doctrine was a modification of the policy of
   (A) isolationism
   (B) watchful waiting
   (C) containment
   (D) massive retaliation

Famous Doctrines in U.S. History, Monroe to Nixon

	Monroe	Truman	Eisenhower	Nixon
Year	1823	1947	1957	1969
Area of World	Western Hemisphere	Greece and Turkey	Middle East	Asia
Reason(s) for Issuance	Feared Spain would try to recolonize Latin America Feared Russian claims on west coast of U.S.	Part of containment strategy Feared Soviet pressure in Greece and Turkey	Designed to block Communism in oil-rich Middle East Feared Soviet moves in the region	Redefined U.S. containment policy, yet reassured allies that U.S. would not retreat to isolationism Responded to U.S. experience in Vietnam
Principles	No new colonies in Western Hemisphere Existing colonies left alone by U.S. U.S. would stay out of European affairs Discouraged the extension of monarchies into Americas	U.S. would provide economic aid to help nations resisting internal or external communist threat	Congress gave president power to provide economic and military aid to nations resisting communist aggression Put Soviets on notice of America's resolve	U.S. would maintain collective security and containment by economic and diplomatic means U.S. would aid allies, but not with American troops
Example of Action	U.S. intervened in Venezuela British boundary dispute in 1895	Sent $400 million to Greece, Turkey	Sent troops to Lebanon in 1958 to restore order and to support America's ally	Gradual removal of U.S. troops from Vietnam (Vietnamization)

Source Activities

Directions: Using the excerpt below and your knowledge of American history, answer the following questions.

> "...the American continents, by the free and independent condition which they have assumed and maintain, are henceforth not to be considered as subjects for future colonization by any European powers...In the wars of the European powers in matters relating to themselves we have never taken any part, nor does it comport with our policy so to do.
>
> ...We owe it, therefore,... to declare that we should consider any attempt on their part [Europe] to extend their system to any portion of this hemisphere as dangerous to our peace and safety. With the existing colonies or dependencies of any European power we have not interfered and shall not interfere...
>
> ...Our policy in regard to Europe...is, not to interfere in the internal concerns of any of its powers; ...It is impossible that the allied powers should extend their political system to any portion of either continent without endangering our peace and happiness..."
>
> —President James Monroe, December, 1823

Multiple-Choice

1. Which of the following efforts most directly resulted from the ideas expressed in the passage?
   - (A) United States intervention into the internal affairs of many Caribbean nations
   - (B) United States refusal to make collective security agreements in the Caribbean
   - (C) United States cooperation with European nations to protect Caribbean nations
   - (D) United States promotion of self-determination in many Caribbean nations

2. The ideas expressed in the passage above most clearly reflect the influence of which of the following?
   - (A) self-determination ideals expressed in the Declaration of Independence
   - (B) isolationist sentiments expressed in the early days of the Republic
   - (C) support for European expansion into the Caribbean after the War of 1812
   - (D) acceptance of free trade agreements with Caribbean nations in the 1820s

Short-Answer

Using the excerpt, answer parts a, b, and c.

a) Briefly outline the main points of President Monroe's 1823 message.

b) Briefly explain how Monroe's ideas influenced ONE of the following twentieth-century policies:
- Big Stick
- Dollar Diplomacy
- Good Neighbor

c) The Monroe Doctrine was both a reflection of continuity as well as change in America's foreign policy toward Latin and South America in the 1820s. Briefly explain ONE important reason EITHER for the change or the continuity expressed in the Doctrine.

Appendices

Appendix A: Answer Key for Multiple-Choice Questions

Use the answer key to see how well you scored on the chart-based multiple-choice questions in each lesson.

Lesson 1: Historical Periods
1. A 2. B 3. D

Lesson 2: Famous Rebellions
1. A 2. D 3. C

Lesson 3: Religious Development, 1619–1740
1. B 2. D 3. D

Lesson 4: Presidents of the United States, 1789–2001
1. C 2. A 3. D

Lesson 5: The First and Second Great Awakenings
1. C 2. A 3. A

Lesson 6: Coming of the American Revolution
1. A 2. C 3. B

Lesson 7: The National Banks
1. D 2. C 3. D

Lesson 8: *Liberal* and *Conservative* in United States History, 1790–1940
1. B 2. D 3. D

Lesson 9: *Liberal* and *Conservative* in United States History, 1940–1985
1. B 2. C 3. D

Lesson 10: Political Parties in the Nineteenth Century
1. A 2. B 3. D

Lesson 11: Third Parties in United States History
1. C 2. D 3. D

Lesson 12: Freedom of the Seas and Wars with Europe
1. A 2. D 3. B

Lesson 13: Compromises and the Union
1. C 2. D 3. A

Lesson 14: Judicial Nationalism, 1819–1824
1. C 2. D 3. B

Lesson 15: Cornerstones of United States Foreign Policy
1. D 2. A 3. C

Lesson 16: Expansion of the United States, 1783–1853
1. B 2. D 3. C

Lesson 17: Wars in United States History
1. D 2. A 3. C

Lesson 18: Amendments to the Constitution
1. A 2. B 3. D

Lesson 19: Utopian Societies in the 1830s and 1840s
1. B **2.** D **3.** A

Lesson 20: Expanding Democracy—The Abolitionist Movement
1. C **2.** D **3.** B

Lesson 21: Women's Movement during the Nineteenth Century
1. D **2.** C **3.** A

Lesson 22: Major Treaties in United States History
1. C **2.** A **3.** D

Lesson 23: Reconstruction of the South
1. D **2.** B **3.** D

Lesson 24: Judicial Betrayal—The Road to *Plessy v. Ferguson*
1. D **2.** D **3.** B

Lesson 25: Monetary Policy—Gold vs. Silver, 1862–1900
1. D **2.** A **3.** D

Lesson 26: Social Darwinism vs. Social Gospel Movement
1. C **2.** A **3.** D

Lesson 27: Black Leaders, 1880–1968
1. B **2.** D **3.** A

Lesson 28: The Supreme Court and Government Regulation, 1890–1937
1. A **2.** C **3.** D

Lesson 29: Reform Movements of the Twentieth Century
1. C **2.** A **3.** B

Lesson 30: Isolationism vs. Internationalism, 1919–1941
1. D **2.** D **3.** B

Lesson 31: Transformation of Capitalism in the 1930s
1. D **2.** A **3.** B

Lesson 32: Presidential Civil Rights Records, 1945–1974
1. C **2.** B **3.** D

Lesson 33: Containment, 1945–1975
1. D **2.** A **3.** C

Lesson 34: Failure of Containment—The Vietnam War
1. D **2.** B **3.** A

Lesson 35: Famous Doctrines—from Monroe to Nixon
1. D **2.** A **3.** C

Appendix A: Answer Key for Multiple Choice Questions

Appendix B

Distribution Charts

Distribution of Items by Chronological Period

Time Periods	Chart & Chart Questions	Source Activities Multiple-Choice	Source Activities Short-Answer	LEQs & DBQs
1600–1754	2.3; 4.1, 2, 3; 5.2, 3	3.1	3.a, b, c	LEQ 1; DBQ 1
1755–1783	6.1, 2, 3; 16.2	6.1, 2	6.a, b, c	
1784–1815	2.2; 3.3; 7.1, 2; 8.1, 2; 10.1, 2; 12.1, 2; 13.1; 18.1	2.1, 2; 3.1, 2; 4.3; 7.2; 12.1, 2; 35.2	2.a, b; 4.a, b, c; 10.a; 12.a	LEQ 2, 3, 4, 8
1816–1837	2.1; 7.3; 13.2; 14.1, 2, 3; 15.1; 20.1, 2; 21.3, 22.1, 35.2	5.1; 10.1, 2; 14.1; 16.1; 25.2; 35.1	5.a, b, c; 7.a, b, c; 10.b; 14.a, b	LEQ 4
1838–1859	1.1; 10.3; 11.2, 3; 16.1, 3; 17.1; 20.3; 19.1, 2, 3; 21.1	5.2; 13.1, 2; 16.2; 18.2; 19.2; 20.1, 2; 21.2; 27.1	13.a, b, c; 16.a, b; 19.a, b, c; 20.a, b, c; 21.a, b	LEQ 4, 6, 8, 9, 16; DBQ 2
1860–1877	4.1, 2; 8.3; 13.3; 18.2; 23.1, 2, 3; 25.3	1.1, 2; 23.1, 2; 32.2	1.a, b, c; 23.a, b	
1878–1901	1.3; 11.1; 15.2, 3; 17.3; 21.2; 24.1, 2, 3; 25.1, 2; 26.1, 2, 3	7.1; 8.1, 2; 11.1, 2; 15.1; 24.1, 2; 25.1; 26.1	8.a, b; 11.a, b, c; 14.c; 23.c; 25.a, b	LEQ 8, 11, 17; DBQ 3
1902–1929	1.2; 12.3; 20.3; 27.3; 30.1, 2, 3; 28.1, 2, 3	15.2; 21.1; 22.1, 2; 28.1; 29.1; 31.2	8.c; 12.b; 15.a, b; 16.c; 21.c; 22.a, b; 26.a, b; 35.b	LEQ 11, 12, 17
1930–1953	8.1; 22.2; 29.2; 31.1, 2, 3; 33.1; 35.1	9.2; 17.1; 18.1; 26.2; 28.2; 30.1, 2; 31.1	15.c; 17.a, b, c; 22.c; 24.a, b, c; 29.a; 30.a, b, c; 31.a, b, c	LEQ 2, 5, 12, 13
1954–1972	8.2; 17.2; 18.3; 27.2; 29.1, 3; 32.1, 2, 3; 33.2, 3; 34.1, 2, 3	14.2; 17.2; 19.1; 27.2; 32.1; 33.1; 34.1, 2	9.b; 27.a, b, c; 29.b, c; 32.a, b, c; 33.a, b; 34.a, b, c	LEQ 14, 15
1973–1990	8.3; 35.3	9.1; 29.2; 33.2	9.a; 33.c	

152 - *Threads of History*

Distribution of Items by Learning Objective

Learning Objective	Source Activities		LEQs & DBQs
	Multiple-Choice	Short-Answer	
POL-1	2.1;		LEQ 1
POL-2	1.1, 2; 2.2; 4.1, 2; 7.1, 2; 10.1, 2; 14.1; 25.2;	2.a, b; 4.a, b, c; 7.a, b, c; 10.a, b;	LEQ 2, 3, 4, 6, 7
POL-3	5.2; 9.2; 19.2; 20.1, 2; 21.2; 27.1; 32.2;	1.a; 20.a, c; 21.a; 23.a, c; 28.a;	LEQ 8, 10, 14; DBQ 2
POL-4	9.1; 29.2;	9.a, b; 29.a, c; 32.b;	LEQ 2, 5, 14
POL-5	13.2; 18.1, 2; 23.1; 24.1, 2; 28.1; 34.1;	13.c; 14.a, b, c; 24.a, c; 28.b;	LEQ 4, 7, 11
POL-6	34.2;	13.a; 34.a, c;	
POL-7	14.2; 27.2; 32.1;	24.c; 27.a, b; 32.a, c;	LEQ 13, 16
ID-1	6.1, 2; 23.2; 35.2;	3.c; 5.a, b, c; 6.a, c; 12.a;	LEQ 1, 8; DBQ 1
ID-2	16.1;	16.b;	LEQ 9
ID-3	31.1;		
ID-7	19.1; 21.1; 28.1;	28.b; 29.b;	
ID-8	14.2; 18.1; 27.2; 32.1;	21.c; 27.c; 32.b;	
CUL-2		19.a, b;	
CUL-4	3.1, 2;		
CUL-5	5.1;		
WOR-3	30.1;	12.b;	LEQ 15
WOR-5	16.2; 35.1;	16.a; 30.b; 35.a, b, c;	
WOR-6	12.1;		
WOR-7	15.1, 2; 17.1, 2; 30.2; 33.1, 2;	15.c; 16.c; 17.a, b, c; 22.a, c; 30.a, c; 33.a, b, c;	LEQ 9, 15, 17
WXT-2	12.2;	19.c;	
WXT-4	13.1;		LEQ 11
WXT-6	25.1; 26.1; 29.1; 31.2;	11.a, c; 25.a; 31.c;	LEQ 12; DBQ 3
WXT-7	11.1, 2;	8.a;	
WXT-8	8.1, 2; 26.2; 28.2; 31.1;	26.a, c; 31.a;	LEQ 12

Explanation of Numbering System:
   "19.1" refers to Lesson 19, multiple-choice question 1.
   "24.a, c" refers to Lesson 24, short-answer question parts a and c.

Appendix B

Distribution Charts

Distribution of Items by Historical Thinking Skill

Skill Type	Historical Thinking Skills	Source Activities		LEQs & DBQs
		Multiple-Choice	Short-Answer	
Chronological Reasoning	Historical Causation	2.2; 3.2; 5.2; 8.2; 9.1; 11.1; 12.1; 14.1; 15.1, 2; 16.2; 17.2; 18.2; 19.2; 20.2; 22.2; 23.1, 2; 24.1; 25.1; 26.1, 2; 27.2; 29.2; 30.2; 31.1; 32.1; 33.1, 2; 34.2; 35.1, 2	2.b; 3.c; 4.a; 5.a, b, c; 8.c; 10.a; 16.b; 19.c; 23.c; 27.c; 30.a, c; 32.a; 33.a; 35.b	LEQ 1, 5, 6, 7, 11, 14, 16; DBQ 1, 2, 3
	Patterns of Continuity and Change over Time	5.1; 7.1, 2; 9.2; 10.1; 11.2; 13.1; 14.2; 16.1; 18.1; 19.1; 21.2; 23.2; 25.2; 26.2; 28.2; 29.1, 2; 30.1; 31.1, 2; 34.1; 35.1	2.a; 7.c; 9.a; 14.c; 16.c; 21.c; 22.c; 35.c	LEQ 1, 4, 5, 6, 7, 8, 12, 14, 15; DBQ 1, 2, 3
	Periodization	1.2;	32.b, c; 33.b	LEQ 9
Comparison and Contextualization	Comparison	4.2; 32.2	12.b; 20.c; 29.b	LEQ 2, 3, 10, 13, 17
	Contextualization	6.2; 10.2; 14.1; 24.2; 30.1; 31.2; 32.2; 33.1	21.c; 22.c; 23.a; 30.c; 33.c	
Crafting Historical Arguments from Historical Evidence	Historical Argumentation		22.a	
	Appropriate Use of Relevant Historical Evidence	1.1; 2.1; 4.1; 3,1; 6.1; 8.1; 12.2; 13.2; 17.1; 20.1; 21.1; 22.1; 24.2; 25.1; 27.1; 28.1	1.a; 4.b, c; 6.a, c; 7.a, b; 9.b; 10.b; 11.a, c; 12.a; 13.a, c; 14.a, b; 15.c; 16.a; 17.a, b, c; 19.a, b, c; 20.a, c; 21.a; 24.a, c; 25.a; 26.a, c; 27.a, b; 28.a, b; 29.a, c; 30.b; 31.a, c; 32.c; 33.c; 34.a, c; 35.a	DBQ 1, 2, 3

154 - *Threads of History*

Applying the Common Core State Standards©

The Common Core State Standards for 11th and 12th grade History and Social Studies revolve entirely around the use of primary and secondary sources, making *Threads* a useful tool for integrating the standards into your existing curriculum. The chart below identifies where each standard is directly addressed in one or more of the practice items; **boldface** indicates that the lesson as a whole addresses the standard in a larger way.

English Language Arts Standards — History and Social Studies, Grades 11–12

Key Ideas and Details:	Lessons
CCSS.ELA-LITERACY.RH.11-12.1 Cite specific textual evidence to support analysis of primary and secondary sources, connecting insights gained from specific details to an understanding of the text as a whole.	1, 4, 6, 7, 12, 13, 14, 17, 19, 21, 24-34
CCSS.ELA-LITERACY.RH.11-12.2 Determine the central ideas or information of a primary or secondary source; provide an accurate summary that makes clear the relationships among the key details and ideas.	4, 7, 14, 16, 20, 22, 23, 27, 30, 35
CCSS.ELA-LITERACY.RH.11-12.3 Evaluate various explanations for actions or events and determine which explanation best accords with textual evidence, acknowledging where the text leaves matters uncertain.	2, 3, 5, 8, 16, 19, 23, 27, 30, 32, 33, 35

Craft and Structure:	Lessons
CCSS.ELA-LITERACY.RH.11-12.4 Determine the meaning of words and phrases as they are used in a text, including analyzing how an author uses and refines the meaning of a key term over the course of a text (e.g., how Madison defines faction in Federalist No. 10).	8, 9, 18, 28
CCSS.ELA-LITERACY.RH.11-12.5 Analyze in detail how a complex primary source is structured, including how key sentences, paragraphs, and larger portions of the text contribute to the whole.	3, 4, 14, 16, **18**, 27, 35
CCSS.ELA-LITERACY.RH.11-12.6 Evaluate authors' differing points of view on the same historical event or issue by assessing the authors' claims, reasoning, and evidence.	5, 10, 11, 15-17, 21, 22, 27, 31, 33, 34

Integration of Knowledge and Ideas:	Lessons
CCSS.ELA-LITERACY.RH.11-12.7 Integrate and evaluate multiple sources of information presented in diverse formats and media (e.g., visually, quantitatively, as well as in words) in order to address a question or solve a problem.	**16**; DBQs 1-3
CCSS.ELA-LITERACY.RH.11-12.8 Evaluate an author's premises, claims, and evidence by corroborating or challenging them with other information.	4, 24, 28, **34**
CCSS.ELA-LITERACY.RH.11-12.9 Integrate information from diverse sources, both primary and secondary, into a coherent understanding of an idea or event, noting discrepancies among sources.	**16**, 19, 28; DBQs 1-3

Range of Reading and Level of Text Complexity:	Lessons
CCSS.ELA-LITERACY.RH.11-12.10 By the end of grade 12, read and comprehend history/social studies texts in the grades 11-CCR text complexity band independently and proficiently.	1-35

Appendix B: Distribution Charts

Appendix C
Worksheets for Primary Sources

Before you try to answer the questions that accompany the written and visual primary source documents, you should first determine what ideas and/or points of view they contain. Below are three simple worksheets for you to use with the primary sources. You can recreate these in your notebook or your teacher may want to reproduce these for you so you have one for each lesson.

Worksheet for Document Source Analysis

Title: _____ What is the title of the document? _____

1. **Date:** _____ When was the document written? _____

2. **Context:** _____ What other events were happening at the time? _____
   _____
   _____

3. **Author:** _____ Who wrote the document? _____
   _____ What was his/her background or position at the time? _____

4. **Message:**

   a. _____ What is it saying? (no more than three or four ideas) _____

   b. _____

   c. _____

   d. _____

156 - *Threads of History*

Worksheet for Visual Source Analysis

Title: _____ What is the title of the visual source? _____

1. **Subject:** _____ What is happening in the visual? _____

   _____

2. **Images:**

   a. _____ Identify three or four images in the visual source. _____

   b. _____

   c. _____

   d. _____

3. **Points:**

   a. What point(s) does the visual make? (no more than three or four ideas)

   b. _____

   c. _____

   d. _____

Appendix C: Worksheets for Primary Sources - 157

Appendix C

Worksheets for Primary Sources

Worksheet for Map Analysis

Title: _____ What is the title of the map? _____

1. **Geography:** _____ What geographic areas are shown? _____

   _____

   _____

2. **Event(s):** _____ What historical event(s) does the map depict? _____

   _____

3. **Benefit(s):**

   a. _____ How does the map increase your knowledge of the event/subject? _____

   b. _____

   c. _____

   d. _____

The answer sheet on the next page is similar to the one you will see on the exam. You can copy this sheet to use for the short-answer questions in the Source Activities, or your teacher may have copies for you.

Please write your short-answer response in the box provided below.

Appendix D

The Mini-Reader

Threads of History provides not only thematic content review, but also serves as a small book of readings and visual sources to accompany your textbook and class notes. It's like two for the price of one! The following is a chronological list of the primary source documents available in this edition of *Threads*:

Year	Page	Type	Topic
1649	12	📄	Puritan Church Platform to the General Court of Massachusetts
1776	26	📄	Loyalist view of the American Revolution
1786	8	📄	George Washington on Shays' Rebellion
1801	18	📄	Thomas Jefferson's First Inaugural Address
1811	52	📄	Felix Grundy and the causes of the War of 1812
1823	60	📄	Reaction to *McCulloch v. Maryland*
1823	146	📄	Monroe Doctrine
1825	43	📄	John Quincy Adams and the role of government
1832	30	📄	Andrew Jackson's veto of the National Bank
1833	86	📄	William Lloyd Garrison and Abolition
1841	82	📄	Constitution of Brook Farm
1845	69	📄	John O'Sullivan and Manifest Destiny
1850	56	📄	John C. Calhoun and the Compromise of 1850
1851	22	✏️	The Second Great Awakening
1853	68	🌐	Expansion of the United States, 1783–1853
1867	98	📄	Thaddeus Stevens and Reconstruction
1868	78	📄	The Fourteenth Amendment
1873	48	✏️	The Granger Movement
1876	4	🌐	The Election of 1876
1883	102	📄	U.S. Civil Rights Cases
1883	110	📄	William Graham Sumner on Social Darwinism

Year	Page	Type	Topic
1894	106	Document	William "Coins" Harvey on Currency Crisis
1894	90	Illustration/Cartoon	Women's Suffrage
1901	34	Document	Theodore Roosevelt and Trusts
1905	118	Document	*Lochner v. U.S.*
1906	64	Illustration/Cartoon	Theodore Roosevelt and the Big Stick Policy
1908	118	Document	*Muller v. Oregon*
1919	94	Illustration/Cartoon	Rejection of the Treaty of Versailles
1935	130	Illustration/Cartoon	New Deal and the Economy
1939	126	Document	Gerald P. Nye and Isolationism
1954	138	Illustration/Cartoon	Containment
1956	74	Document	Harry Truman and the Korean War
1957	134	Document	President Eisenhower and Little Rock Crisis
1964	38	Document	Barry Goldwater's acceptance speech
1964	122	Document	Lyndon Johnson's War on Poverty
1964	114	Document	Malcolm X on Civil Rights Movement
1969	142	Photograph	Vietnam Protest

Reader Key:
- Document
- Map
- Illustration/Cartoon
- Photograph

Notes

Notes

Notes

Notes

SHERPALEARNING
GUIDING YOU TO EVEN GREATER HEIGHTS

Our mission is to open doors for high-achieving learners through access to high-quality, skills-based instruction written by rock-star teachers.

Threads of History — 2nd Edition

Teacher Edition

- 10 detailed Lesson Plans based on topics/themes introduced in 10 of the Review Activities guide you to use *Threads* to its full potential; designed to be completed in a 50 minute class period
- Distribution Charts to help you integrate *Threads* into your existing curriculum and design custom quizzes and assignments
- Complete answers and explanations for the Source Activities
- Suggested responses for the 17 Long Essay Questions and 3 Document-Based Questions
- Rubrics and rubric helpers that Mike has presented in workshops across the country

ISBN: 978-0-9905471-1-2

Teacher Companion Website

- 17 Long Essay Questions in the new exam format
- 3 original Document-Based Questions
- H.I.P.P.O. DBQ Planning Worksheet
- 150+ Multiple-Choice review questions that you can use to assemble custom quizzes and tests, with detailed answer analysis
- Core Chart Worksheets for building students' synthesis and summarization skills
- Printable worksheets and answer sheets designed to simulate the exam format
- More resources will continue to be added as they become available

Go to **threads.sherpalearning.com** to register

Note to Teachers and Administrators

We at Sherpa Learning hope to continue to create amazing content at sensible prices for years to come. But we're a small crew of believers with no corporate umbrella to hide under. As such, we'd ask that you consider buying a class set if you can afford it. We understand that times are tough and that sometimes you just have to do what you have to do. The students come first. But it's hard for a company like ours to survive selling one book at a time. Just keep it in mind. That's all we ask.

And if you loved this book, check out our site for other amazing resources. Don't forget to register with the site to be informed of new products and promotions as they become available.

www.sherpalearning.com